BATTERY B

The diary of a soldier
In a volunteer artillery battery
And a big and bloody war

Robert Smiley Dunnan
American Civil War
1861-1862

David Butt

DAVID BUTT

ISBN 978-0-9923037-1-6

Copyright © 2013 David Butt
Second edition   March 2014

All rights reserved. Because of the dynamic nature of the Internet, any Web addresses or links contained in this book may have changed since publication and may no longer be valid.

Editorial work by Dana McCown and Bob McCown

storybridge press
Brisbane, Queensland, Australia

Front and back cover design by Sam McCown

DEDICATION

This book is dedicated to
Willard Dunnan McCown
who helped keep alive the history of the
Dunnan family in Western Pennsylvania,
in his generation and beyond.

DAVID BUTT

Leather-bound diary and Colt revolver belonging to Robert Dunnan; Call to Arms in Western Pennsylvania following the seizure of Fort Sumter; *History of Pennsylvania Volunteers, 1861-1865* (Samuel P. Bates); Lapel button worn by three-year veterans. See also p162.
Items not displayed in accurate proportion

ACKNOWLEDGEMENTS

Much of the material on which this publication is based comes from two key historical works. The first – **History of Pennsylvania Volunteers, 1861-65,** by Samuel P. Bates, published in Harrisburg, Pa, by the State Printer in 1869 – is testament to the visionary decision of the Pennsylvania Legislature to provide a military history of the organization, and services in the field, of each regiment, and information as far as possible on each person who served in the Pennsylvania volunteers. The history of the 1st Artillery, or 43rd Regiment, is contained in Volume I of this series, and provides specific information on Battery B. Operating in the post-war reconstruction period, when much of the information which would subsequently be released through the Official Records was not as yet public, Bates did an extraordinary job in trawling through all the information available, including individual accounts which he sought from war participants, and compiling what remains a very enjoyable and well documented history.

The second -- the Official Records (**The War of the Rebellion: A Compilation of the Official Records of the Federal and Confederate Armies)** – provides in-depth information on the American Civil War: detail which for its time was unparalleled in the history of war. This includes insights into the role of Battery B within the Union Army, along with that of its Regiment, Brigade, Division, and Corps. The ORs do this within the context of the bigger picture of the progress of the war in the East, including correspondence between President Abraham Lincoln and his field commanders.

Likewise the fields of Gettysburg proved fertile (as well as hallowed) ground: the address of Battery B's 1st Lieutenant James A. Gardner at the 1889 dedication of the Battery B monument on Cemetery Hill both commemorates their exploits over the course of those historic three days, as well as giving further historical background on the Battery.

Much credit also goes to the Library of Congress for its marvelous success in compiling its online catalog of publications, including photographs, maps and other illustrations. This proved an invaluable collection and source of material, including for the illustrations which adorn these pages.

The historical website on *Pennsylvania in the Civil War* – http://www.pa-roots.com/pacw/index.html -- also was a very valuable aid in providing directions to relevant material.

More broadly, the navigation access provided by the internet, and the quick access to background material from Wikipedia, which helped identify directions to be pursued to access relevant material, was a major aid, particularly for someone working on this subject from so far away.

Acknowledgement of other source material is footnoted throughout the publication.

Closer to home, I want to sincerely thank Dana McCown for voluntarily taking charge of knocking the publication into shape. It was a huge amount of work. Bob McCown not only helped with this process but painstakingly worked through the indexing. I am sure neither knew how much work was involved. It was indeed a labor of love.

General-in-Chief George McClellan (centre) and his Union Generals in 1861

CONTENTS

Acknowledgements	v
Maps	ix
Illustrations	x
Preface	xiii
Introduction	xvi
The Soldier	xvi
The Battery	xix
The Making of an Artillery Regiment…	xix
…and of the Pennsylvania Reserves	xxii
The War	xxvii
Chronology	xxxi
The diary – The story	1
General George McClellan	3
General George McCall	5
General John Reynolds	5
General George Meade	24
Joint Committee on Conduct of War	35
The Valley Campaign Part 1	50
The Peninsula Campaign Part 1	55
The Valley Campaign Part 2	59
The Peninsula Campaign Part 2	63
Battle of Hanover Court House	63
Battle of Seven Pines	66
And finally: The Reserves head to the Peninsula	69
The Peninsula Campaign Part 3:	76
The *Seven Days Battles*	76
Battle of Oak Grove	76
Battle of Beaver Dam Creek	78
Battle of Gaines's Mill	88
Battle of Garnett's and Golding's Farms	99
Battle of Savage's Station	100
Battle of Glendale	102
Battle of Malvern Hill	120
The End	121
Postscript	125
Appendices	127
A. The Aftermath	127

General George McClellan	127
General George McCall	129
General George Meade	129
General John Reynolds	131
Captain James Cooper	133
The Dunnan Soldiers	137
Samuel Dunnan	137
John Dunnan	137
James Dunnan	137
Hugh Dunnan	138
B. Letter on return of Robert Dunnan's personal effects	140
C. Official Army records of the Dunnan brothers in Battery B	141
D. Battery B engagements 1861-65	142
E. Roll of Honor	143
F. Dedication of the monument at Gettysburg	145
G. Association of Battery B	163
H. New Castle News: obituary for Captain James Cooper	167
I. Civil War Army Organization and Rank	171
J. Orders of Battle / Seven Days Battles	175
Index	178

Battery B Monument base at Mt Jackson Battery B Cemetery

MAPS

Trail showing the journey of Private Dunnan and Battery B in 1861-62	xxxiii
Map of Lower Peninsula of Virginia	55
Journey of Battery B in *Seven Days Battles*	75
Plan of *Battle of Beaver Dam Creek*	87
Plan of *Battle of Gaines's Mill*	98
Plan of *Battle of Glendale*	118/119

V Corps' General Fitz John Porter (seated) with officers and staff at Harrison's Landing, August, 1862. Private Dunnan and Battery B served in V Corps during the *Seven Days Battles*.

ILLUSTRATIONS

Robert's diary and revolver with Civil War artefacts	iv
General-in-Chief George McClellan and his Union commanders	vi
Battery B Monument at Mt. Jackson	viii
V Corps' Porter and staff at Harrison's Landing, August, 1862	ix
Robert Dunnan's gravestone at Glendale Military Cemetery	xii
Artillery in front of Camp Barry	xv
Original flag for the Pennsylvania Reserves 1st Artillery	xviii
Captain James H. Cooper, Battery B commander	xxi
Cooper's Battery B in action before Petersburg 1864 (1)	xxiv
Cooper's Battery B in action before Petersburg 1864 (2)	xxv
1st Pennsylvania Infantry Reserves in camp	xxvi
Answering the call to arms	xxx
Camp life for the 2nd Pennsylvania Regiment	xxxii
Page from diary	xxxiv
Arsenal in Washington	2
Camp Tenallytown in 1864	2
General George B. McClellan	3
General George A. McCall	6
General John F. Reynolds	6
Troops on parade on Pennsylvania Avenue, Washington	7
Washington D.C. barracks and arsenal	9
Great Falls Soldiers and civilians	10
Washington Aqueduct	12
Aqueduct Bridge over the Potomac	12
Parrott rifles: key weapons for Battery B	14
Lowe's hot air balloon and gas generators	17
Parrott Rifle	19
General Charles P. Stone and daughter	23
General George G. Meade	24
Troops of the Pennsylvanian Reserves 7th Regiment	25
General William Barry	26
General Edward Ord and family	31
The Chain Bridge during the Civil War	33
General Charles Stone	35
"Bodies in the Potomac after Ball's Bluff" by Alfred R. Waud	36
Secretary of War Edwin Stanton	38

Howitzer	42
I Corps' Irvin McDowell	44
II Corps' Edwin Sumner	44
III Corps' Samuel Heintzelman	44
IV Corps' Erasmus Keyes	44
General Truman Seymour	45
General Joseph E. Johnston	46
General Thomas "Stonewall" Jackson	54
Confederate General "Prince John" Magruder	56
Turret and deck of the *U. S. S. Monitor*	58
General Richard S. Ewell	61
VI Corps' William Franklin	63
1st Division's Henry Slocum	63
2nd Division's William Smith	63
V Corps' Fitz John Porter	64
1st Division's George Morrell	64
2nd Division's George Sykes	64
3rd Division's George McCall	64
"Battle of Hanover Court House" by Alfred R Waud	65
Artillery battery with 3-inch ordinance guns	67
General Robert E. Lee	68
White House Landing	71
Transports at White House Landing	72
Soldiers of the 2nd Regiment in Reynolds's 1st Brigade	74
Confederate General Benjamin Huger	77
Confederate Generals A. P. Hill & D. H. Hill	79
Colonel William "Buck" McCandless	82
Major Roy Stone	82
Confederate Generals Anderson, Archer, Field, Pender and Ripley	85
Ellerson's Mill at Beaver Dam Creek	87
Confederate Generals Gregg and Branch	92
Union Generals Martindale, Griffin and Butterfield	95
Harper's Weekly: *"Battery fire at Gaines's Mill"*	96
Confederate General John Hood at Gaines's Mill	97
Grapevine Bridge across the Chickahominy	97
Savage's Station before the battle	101
Wounded men after the *Battle of Savage's Station*	101
General Joseph Hooker	104
General Phillip Kearny	104

Battery Captain Alanson Randol	105
Colonel Seneca Simmons	105
Confederate Generals Jenkins, Wilcox and Kemper	107
Colonel (later General) C. Feger Jackson	108
Major General John Sedgwick	111
An 1864 engraving of the battle for McCall's artillery at Glendale	116
White Oak Swamp; and White Oak Swamp Bridge destroyed	117
Chief of Artillery Henry Hunt	120
Union Officers at Malvern Hill, July, 1862	124
Wounded soldiers in a Union hospital	126
General John Sedgwick at Harrison's Landing	126
Lincoln in McClellan's tent after the *Battle of Antietam*	128
General George Meade and staff	131
"The Fall of Reynolds" by Alfred R. Waud	133
"Coopers Arty" by Alfred R. Waud	136
Pontoons across James River	139
Letter from Sgt. Samuel Dunnan to brother Hugh Dunnan	140
Official Army records of the Dunnan Brothers from Battery B	141
Union Veterans Lapel Button	162
Dedication of the Mount Jackson Battery B Monument	164
Monument at the Mt Jackson Battery B Cemetery	166
"Battle of Malvern Hill" by R.K. Sneden	176
General John H. Martindale near Richmond	176
Drawing by Waud of Pennsylvanian Reserves last battle	177
Alanson Randol	177
Heintzelman and staff at Harrisons Landing	177

Robert's gravestone at Glendale National Military Cemetery
His middle initial was incorrectly recorded as C instead of S.

PREFACE

This story has been more than 150 years in the making.

It started in 1861 in the early days of the American Civil War when a young private from Western Pennsylvania arrived in Washington and decided to purchase a small, leather-bound diary. In it he kept a brief, irregular record of the first year of a war which for him, and for so many others like him, was beyond anything he ever could have imagined – a war which stands as the most defining period in American history.

That private, Robert Dunnan, died in the war and after his death his older brother, Samuel, who was serving in the same unit as Robert (along with his youngest brother, John), sent Robert's diary and revolver back to the family on the farm at Mt Jackson, Lawrence County, in Pennsylvania.

The diary and revolver were passed down through John Dunnan's descendants to grandson Willard Dunnan McCown and then to Willard's sons, Bob (diary) and Dan (revolver).

The diary went to Australia with Bob and his young family in the 1960s where it remained in safe keeping for the next 40 years, with Bob managing to painstakingly transcribe a number of pages in the 1980s. In December, 2012, Bob came across the diary and the partial transcription. Thinking that the next generations of Australians might be interested, he showed it around at the family Christmas gathering in Brisbane – a long way from the Civil War battlefields. And indeed it was interesting, so as Bob's son-in-law I offered to transcribe the remainder. Little did I realize that this would evolve into an old-fashioned "commission" as "the authority" to write a book around Robert's diary[1].

The faded pencil entries with their phonetic spelling of words and colloquial usage had become increasingly difficult to decipher. But I persevered and ended up with a sketchy record of less than 4,000 words about where Robert Dunnan had been and what he had seen. It was not much to go on. However there were dates, there were towns

---

[1] Commission: *archaic* – the authority to carry out a task (Concise Oxford English Dictionary).

and rivers, there were brief descriptions of battles. And to my intrigue the diary was peppered with interesting names like "Lincoln", "Stanton", "McClellan", "McCall", "Meade" and "Reynolds". Oh, and a man named "Cooper". But more on him later.

An initial search started to join the dots and I began to realize what I had on my hands. Very soon it became apparent that those short diary entries linked Robert Dunnan to some of the bigger stories of the war – of Presidents and personalities, of politics and Army commanders, of skirmishes and battles, of wins, draws and losses -- of intense savagery, bloodshed, pain and suffering.

After considerably more research, I have aimed to piece together the story of Robert Dunnan and the battery in which he served – Battery B, 1st Light Artillery of the Pennsylvania Reserves – of where it went and why, and importantly of the bigger picture of the war in which it was engulfed.

My aim has been to bring Robert's story to life – to present his diary entries, and alongside or below those entries, his story and that of Battery B within the overall context of the war – and thereby to bring to life the stories of the thousands of others who lived and died like Private Dunnan.

For certainly I have found it a fascinating juxtaposition. In his simply told story, Robert Dunnan makes no attempt to interpret what was going on around him – no analysis of the big battles, of the strategy behind the orders that he willingly followed, and certainly not of the political overlay both within the Union and more broadly between the North and the South.

His is a simple tale written in a firm bold hand, with the spelling owing much to the spoken word of those around him. He says little of his battery colleagues, does not even mention the two brothers who were there fighting beside him, and attributes deeds of bravery to no one, despite all that he clearly witnessed.

Yet however uncomplicated Robert Dunnan's story appears, with the seemingly aimless marching and counter marching across Maryland and Virginia, of moving from camp to camp, of being ordered to standby to march and then being stood down without explanation, Robert's diary provides a pathway for much of the bigger story of the war in the Eastern Zone and how it unfolded in those vital first 12 months. Seemingly innocuous diary entries take on new meaning when they are looked at in the knowledge of what was happening at the time in the overall theatre of the war in the East, in that area surrounding the 100 miles between rival capitals Washington and Richmond.

Sometimes Private Dunnan's story runs parallel to the action, sometimes it is just over the hill or a short march away, sometimes the two come together violently. It is always there, lurking, deadly, just beyond or buried within a few short sharp words written in pencil in his yellowed, well-worn notebook.

This is a short, simple story written by a young farmer and framed within a momentous, hostile and transformational time in American history. It is the story of a soldier, a volunteer artillery battery and a nation-defining war.

David Butt

Artillery in front of Camp Barry near Washington

INTRODUCTION

THE SOLDIER

Robert Dunnan's father, John Dunnan, was born near Belfast in County Down, Ireland, in 1764 and immigrated to America as a young man. After a time in New York, John Dunnan moved to Chambersburg in Franklin County, Pennsylvania, where he married Betty Chambers, the sister of the founder of the town, Benjamin Chambers. When Betty died, John Dunnan moved first to Washington County in Western Pennsylvania and then to North Beaver Township, which at that time was a part of Beaver County (it became part of the new Lawrence County in 1849). There he married Ann Smiley, the daughter of a Scottish pioneer named Hugh Smiley and a woman 37 years younger than him who was born on a farm two miles from Wurtemburg, on the New Castle Road, in Lawrence County.

John (1764-1846) and Ann (1801-1876) raised eight children on their farm near Mt Jackson: John N. Dunnan (1826-1837), David Dunnan (1828-1837), James Alexander Dunnan (1830-1904), Samuel Dunnan (1832-1922), Robert Smiley Dunnan (1834-1862), Martha Smiley Dunnan (1836-1912), Hugh Dunnan (1839-1909), and John Dunnan (1842-1923).

By the time of the Civil War, the first two sons had died in childhood, while John Dunnan Senior had also passed away, aged 82. Then in 1861, the life of the Dunnans and millions of others like them was changed abruptly. After a long build-up of tension between the North and the South over States rights, brought to a head by the North's move to abolish slavery and the election of Abraham Lincoln as President, southern States began to secede from the Union. The South had what they thought was a very logical view on secession: the States had ceded certain powers and authorities to the Federal Government to enable the creation of the Union, and seceding was the exercising of those same State rights to withdraw those powers and authorities.

The North rejected that rationale: the maintenance of the United States was seen as paramount. As tensions increased, war became inevitable.

On April 12, 1861, the first shots in what became the American Civil War were fired in the battle for Fort Sumter off Charleston, South Carolina. With Federal troops forced to withdraw from Fort Sumter on April 14, and fearful of an invasion of Washington, on April 15, Lincoln called for 75,000 "loyal citizens" to join the United States volunteers.

The response was overwhelming. Young men rushed forward to join, willing to fight to maintain the National Union, while also looking for action and adventure, and fearful they might miss out in what was expected to be a short-fought war (the initial call for States to provide volunteer militia was on the basis that they join up "for three months, or sooner, if discharged").

In a letter written in 1960 to her niece, Susan Whitney (Hugh Dunnan's great granddaughter), Mary Elizabeth Dunnan (James Alexander Dunnan's daughter and by then 92 years old) told of how all of the Dunnan sons wanted to volunteer. James had moved to Iowa before the war and the four brothers remaining in Mt Jackson – Samuel, Robert, Hugh and John – were all keen to enlist. But someone had to stay at home to help their widowed mother with the farm, and it was decided that, as the youngest son, it should be John.

"That did not please him so he got up very early next morning and had already been enrolled in Co. B. Mt Jackson Volunteers when the other boys got there. The food for soldiers was just as important as men, so after a hurried consultation, it was decided the next youngest, your great-grandfather Hugh, should run the farm until one of them shuld (sic) come back. He did so for three years until John's term of enlistment ended."

At the time he enlisted, Robert Dunnan was 26 and had a dark complexion and dark hair, with blue eyes. He was 5 feet 10½ inches tall, and registered his occupation as a carpenter living in Mt Jackson, Pennsylvania.

His brother, Samuel, 28, had similar features to Robert's although he was shorter at 5 feet 8½ inches. He too was recorded as a carpenter from Mt Jackson. On August 2, before they had reached Washington, Samuel was promoted to Corporal.

DAVID BUTT

John, 19, was of a light complexion with dark hair and blue eyes, 5 feet 9 inches tall, and was recorded as a farmer from Mt Jackson.

Older brother James, 31, enlisted in Company G of the 3rd Iowa Cavalry Volunteers on August 26, 1861.

Hugh remained on the farm until John returned in 1864 and then in September that year, by then aged 25, enlisted in Company B, 5th Regiment, Pennsylvania Heavy Artillery (204th Volunteers).

Thus like so many other American families at that time, in both the North and the South, ultimately all of the Dunnan brothers went off to war.

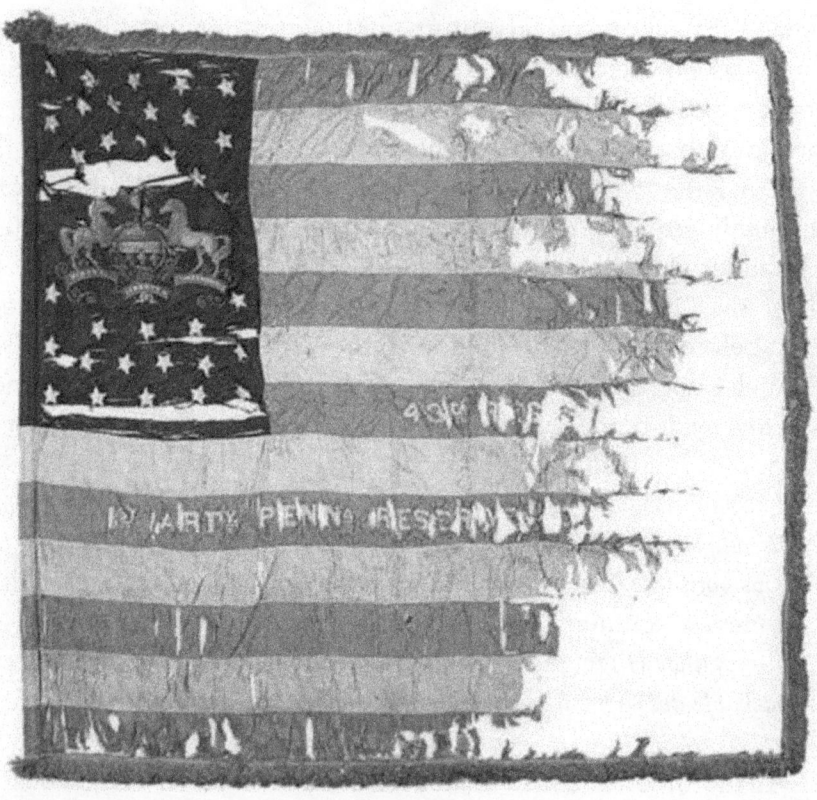

Original flag of the 1st Light Artillery Regiment, Pennsylvania Reserves (43rd Regiment) – the flag Battery B fought under. The flag, which has the Pennsylvania State seal over the US flag, is in the collection of the Pennsylvania Capital Preservation Committee in Harrisburg, Pa.[2]

---

[2]http://cpc.state.pa.us/flags/flag-search.cfm (Click to show all.)

THE BATTERY
The Making of an Artillery Regiment...

[3]As war broke out, the call went out across Pennsylvania for volunteers for a Light Artillery Regiment. On April 22, a meeting was held at Mt Jackson, where plans were drawn up for a unit to be known as the Mt Jackson Guards. The following day, circulars calling for volunteers were posted throughout Lawrence County and, on April 26, what later became Battery B was formally organized at Mount Jackson, "composed mainly of farmers' sons, business men and school teachers, all in the prime and vigor of manhood; from a locality unexcelled in thrift and in the intelligence and religious culture of its inhabitants."[4]

In all, 78 recruits from the local community signed up that day. They included brothers, relatives and friends from the early pioneering families of the county, most of whom had rarely travelled far from their farms and small communities. Many families had two brothers in those first ranks: others like the Dunnans contributed three brothers. Four members of the Shaffer family – German pioneers to Mt Jackson – enlisted (one would subsequently die of disease, another was killed at *Second Bull Run*, and a third was wounded at both *Second Bull Run* and the *Battle of Gettysburg*). Henry T. Danforth,

---

[3] Key sources for the historical information provided in this publication include:
- *History of Pennsylvania Volunteers, 1861-65*, by Samuel P. Bates, published in Harrisburg, Pa, by the State Printer in 1869. The history of the 43rd Regiment, 1st Artillery, is contained in Volume I of this series, and provides specific information on Battery B;
- *The War of the Rebellion: A Compilation of the Official Records of the Federal and Confederate Armies:* where cited specifically, the abbreviation OR is used for Official Records, along with Volume, Part, Chapter and page/s. All citations are from Series I.

[4] Address by First Lieutenant James A. Gardner at the September 11, 1889, dedication of the monument to Battery B on Cemetery Hill, Gettysburg. See also Appendix F.

34, who previously served with distinction in a regular artillery battery in the Mexican war (1846-1848), was the Battery's first captain.

Initially, the State did not have the authority to accept the Mt Jackson volunteers as militia (along with thousands of others like them from across the State). But following the passage of State legislation enabling the creation of the Pennsylvania Reserves in May, 1861, the Battery was entered into the Pennsylvania State service on June 8, 1861. The 78 men then assembled at the Methodist Episcopal Church in Mt Jackson and began the march to the train station at Enon Valley. As they marched they were met by farmers who hitched up their wagons and gave them a lift to the station and from there they caught a train to Camp Wright near Pittsburgh. There they were joined by a further 10 men from Western Pennsylvania and were formally mustered in on June 28. On July 22 – the day after the Union defeat at *First Bull Run* – they embarked from Pittsburgh for Camp Curtin at Harrisburg, Pa, (named after the State Governor Andrew Curtin) and another six men joined their ranks.

At Camp Curtin, the Battery joined with three other companies recruited in the counties of Franklin, Potter, York and Luzerne, and four Philadelphian companies to form the 1st Light Artillery, Pennsylvania Reserve Corps. The regiment was clothed and equipped by the State of Pennsylvania, and received arms from the State and from the City of Philadelphia.

On August 7, the regiment was ordered to Washington, and further recruits would join them over the following months to give them the manpower required for the battery – about 100 men when it was a four gun battery and 150 when it had six guns. On reaching the capital, Danforth, who had been promoted from Captain to Major on August 1 (and would subsequently become Lieutenant Colonel), was ordered to duty with batteries in a separate Division engaged in the fortification of Washington. Wanting to see action with the battery which he had helped recruit, in December that year Danforth resigned his commission and enlisted as a private in the ranks with his old companions in Battery B. He was immediately elected a Second Lieutenant and placed in charge of one of two (and later three) gun sections within the battery (each section contained two guns). Danforth's experience and expertise were no doubt key contributors to Battery B's highly lethal and effective performance in battle.

With Danforth's departure as Battery commander, a new commander was appointed – one whose name would become forever entwined in the legend of the exploits of Battery B. Captain James H. (Harvey) Cooper (1840-1906), one of the original volunteers in the Mt Jackson Guards, was just 21 years old when he was promoted from First Sergeant to Second Lieutenant on June 28, 1861, and then to Captain of the Battery on August 2, 1861. For more than three years, until he was mustered out on August 8, 1864, Cooper served as commander of Battery B – or what became known and has since been commemorated as *Cooper's Battery*.

Battery B commander, Captain James Harvey Cooper

...and of the Pennsylvania Reserves

President Lincoln's call of April 15, 1861, for 75,000 State militia to suppress the southern revolt had a galvanizing effect – for both the North and the South.

In the South, among States which had not yet seceded, there was outrage that they were being asked to provide troops to fight against their southern colleagues. This drove four more States to secede and join the Confederacy – Virginia, Tennessee, Arkansas, and North Carolina.

In the North, men from all over the countryside came forward to enlist. Pennsylvania had been asked to provide 16 regiments, including two to be provided within three days due to fears of an attack on Washington. Very quickly, five volunteer militia companies, which had been training in readiness for an anticipated war, were dispatched and, after working their way through a hostile crowd in Baltimore, their 530 troops were the first to arrive to aid in guarding the capital.

Ultimately Pennsylvania easily exceeded its quota of 16 regiments in response to Lincoln's initial call for three-month volunteers. These regiments served a variety of roles. Some were engaged in the defense of Washington, in both providing a deterrent force and building up the city's defenses. Others were sent to the vital Border States of Maryland and Delaware to keep the peace among the populations, prevent those disloyal to the North from advocating for secession, and block the sending of troops and supplies to the rebel army. The threat of Maryland seceding, which would have isolated Washington, remained a risk until May when Union troops took control of Baltimore and martial law was declared. Still more regiments were sent to protect against Confederate troops who were massing near Harpers Ferry in the Shenandoah Valley from crossing the Potomac River from Virginia into Maryland and from there threatening Pennsylvania's southern border.

Most of these initial regiments saw little action between being mustered in and by the time many of the regiments were mustered out three months later (some of them were mustered in for three years, and many of the men mustered out re-enlisted in different regiments).

Concerned about the short three-month duration of service for the initial volunteers, and for the defense of Pennsylvania from attack, the commander of the Pennsylvanian troops, General Robert Patterson, made a requisition on Pennsylvanian Governor Andrew Curtin for additional regiments to be formed, and the Governor put out the call for extra forces. When the national authorities learnt of this, they advised the forces were not needed and ordered that the call be countermanded. But it was already too late: companies and regiments were forming across the State.

Still concerned about the potential danger to Pennsylvania, and recognizing the State did not have the legislative authority to proceed with the creation of an army to protect itself, on April 20, 1861, Governor Curtin issued a proclamation calling for the passage of laws to enable the organizing, disciplining and arming of Pennsylvanian regiments "exclusive of those called into the service of the United States." On May 15, new laws came into effect which required the formation of a military corps to be called the "Reserve Volunteer Corps of the Commonwealth" and which was to be composed of thirteen regiments of infantry, one regiment of cavalry, and one regiment of light artillery.

Thus was born the Pennsylvania Reserves.

The Reserves was made up of 12 infantry regiments (1st to the 12th Reserves Regiments), the 1st Pennsylvania Rifles (13th Reserves, but commonly called the "Bucktails"), the 1st Pennsylvania Light Artillery (14th Reserves, which included Battery B), and the 1st Pennsylvania Cavalry (15th Reserves). Later they were renamed the 30th to 44th Volunteer Regiments (the 1st Artillery was named the 43rd Volunteer Regiment) to align with the naming convention of other Pennsylvanian regiments, but the original names remained in common use throughout the war and indeed in historical Orders of Battle.

George A. McCall was appointed Major General in charge of the Corps, and training camps were set up to prepare the recruits for war.

With the defeat at Bull Run on July 21, the Union Army found itself pushed back to the gates of Washington. With many of the Army's troops due to be mustered out at the end of their three months' service, an immediate call went out to the States for assistance. Because of their foresight in organizing the Reserves, Pennsylvania was able to respond immediately.

DAVID BUTT

Cooper's Battery B in action before Petersburg, 1864. In this and the next photograph, a bearded Cooper is seen leaning on his sword, – in the one on this page left of center in a slightly raised position in the middle of the group behind the first cannon, and in the one on the next page in the foreground slightly to the left of center

BATTERY B

These photographs were taken by war photographer Mathew Brady who obtained permission to take a picture of Cooper's Battery in position for battle. When the Confederates saw them form up, they opened fire and Brady's horse ran off with his wagon and his assistant, upsetting and destroying his chemicals.

The Pennsylvania Reserves were formed as a Division made up of three Brigades under McCall's command in the Army of the Potomac in Washington in August, 1861.

The 13 infantry regiments of the Pennsylvania Reserves fought as the only army division all from a single state. For much of the following three years many of the Reserves regiments – along with a number of Batteries from the 1st Artillery Regiment, and most regularly Battery B – fought side by side throughout many of the most important battles of the war. They suffered and inflicted heavy casualties throughout the war, and developed an enviable reputation for their performance in battle, as well as for producing some of the most important leaders in the Union Army.

Most of the regiments were mustered out in May and June, 1864, after their three-year service expired. A large number of the men then re-enlisted, becoming the 190th and 191st Pennsylvania Volunteers, and fought until the end of the war.

Ultimately Pennsylvania provided 215 volunteer regiments and 360,000 men to the war effort.

1st Pennsylvania Infantry Reserves in camp

THE WAR

In the beginning, the strongly-held view from both the North and the South was that the war would be all over within 90 days. Then on July 21, 1861, as the Dunnan brothers were at Camp Wright in Pittsburgh preparing for life in the artillery, that belief was dashed by the *First Battle of Bull Run*.

First Bull Run (or *First Manassas* as it was known by the Confederates) was the first major land battle of the American Civil War and came about more because of public pressure for urgent action rather than any organized strategic battle plan from the Union leadership. Smarting from their loss at Fort Sumter, the Northern public and its political leaders were demanding a march against the Confederate capital of Richmond, Virginia, which they expected would bring an early end to the rebellion.

Yielding to that pressure, the commander of the Army of Northeastern Virginia, Brigadier General Irvin McDowell, led his inexperienced and under-prepared Union Army across the waters of Bull Run. McDowell faced the equally inexperienced Confederate Army of his former West Point colleague, Brigadier General P. G. T. Beauregard, camped near Manassas Junction in Prince William County, Virginia, about 30 miles from Washington.

McDowell's battle plans were poorly executed by his untried troops but still met with some initial success. If the battle had run its course without further intervention, the Union may have won the day. But this was a time of technological change and, for the first (but not the last) time in the war, the railroad system played a major role in the outcome of the battle. Confederate Brigadier General Joseph E. Johnston was able to use the rail system to bring reinforcements up quickly to the battlefields from the Shenandoah Valley, and the battle quickly swung against the Union.

A brigade of Virginians under a colonel from the Virginia Military Institute, Thomas J. Jackson, stood its ground and thus Jackson received his famous nickname, "Stonewall". The Confederates then launched a strong counterattack, aided by their superior use of artillery. As the Union troops began withdrawing under fire, major problems were encountered crossing back over Bull Run. Many panicked and it turned into a rout as McDowell's men frantically ran towards Washington.

The battle resulted in casualties and losses for the North of 2,896 (460 killed, 1,124 wounded, and 1,312 captured or missing) and 1,982 for the South (387 killed, 1,582 wounded and 13 missing).

The South was elated, albeit somewhat sobered by the realization that the type of war being waged could result in massive casualties. For the North, the loss was devastating, both for the Army and for the morale of the population. Quick victory had been thought to be so certain that many spectators had come to watch, only to have to join in (and indeed impede) the panicked retreat. The Union was crumbling, the national capital was in danger and there was a growing realization of the potential for a long, drawn-out and bloody war which the North could lose.

Two Union Generals took much of the blame for defeat. Pennsylvanian General Robert Patterson was highly criticized for failing to act against the Confederate forces in the Shenandoah Valley, enabling Confederate General Johnston to move unopposed to reinforce his colleagues, and turn the tide of battle. Within days, Patterson was mustered out of the army. Irvin McDowell also was blamed for his poor command on the battlefield and President Lincoln shortly afterwards replaced him with Major General George B. McClellan who would later be named General-in-Chief of all the Union armies.

In a memorandum to Lincoln dated August 4, 1861, General McClellan described his view of the consequences of the loss at Bull Run and the inevitable type of war which he considered would need to be fought and won -- not simply to defeat the South but to crush their forces and any will to resist:

"The object of the present war differs from those in which nations are usually engaged mainly in this, that the purpose of ordinary war is to conquer a peace and make a treaty on advantageous terms. In this contest it has become necessary to crush a population sufficiently numerous, intelligent, and warlike to constitute a nation. We have not only to defeat their armed and organized forces in the field, but to display such an overwhelming strength as will convince all our antagonists, especially those of the governing, aristocratic class, of the utter impossibility of resistance. Our late reverses make this course imperative. Had we been

successful in the recent battle (Manassas), it is possible that we might have been spared the labor and expenses of a great effort. Now we have no alternative. Their success will enable the political leaders of the rebels to convince the mass of their people that we are inferior to them in force and courage, and to command all their resources. The contest began with a class; now it is with a people. Our military success can alone restore the former issue. By thoroughly defeating their armies, taking their strong places, and pursuing a rigidly protective policy as to private property and unarmed persons, and a lenient course as to private soldiers, we may well hope for a permanent restoration of a peaceful Union. But in the first instance the authority of the Government must be supported by overwhelming physical force."[5]

Four years of ferocious and bloody battles followed, resulting in massive casualties in what might be described as the forerunner to modern warfare as it is known today. It involved the use of rifled guns and cannons enabling vastly improved accuracy of propelled bullets and shells over long distances, as well as the forerunner to the Gatling gun and thus the machine gun (the coffee-mill gun). The new ability to move troops rapidly by train provided for significantly enhanced battle mobility. Ciphered telegraph messaging enabled rapid long-distance communications between Army commanders, and between the commanders and their political leaders. This in turn created the best record ever held of the progress of a war – a major source for the Official Records. The Civil War also produced the first iron clad battleships and even a submarine, as well as air support (balloons used both for observation and for directing artillery fire) and the world's first aircraft carrier (p. 17).

It was into this environment, in the aftermath of Bull Run, that Private Robert Dunnan and Battery B arrived with their regiment in Washington – to a city reeling from defeat, poorly defended, and in fear of attack.

---

[5] OR, Volume 5, Chapter XIV, p6

Answering the call to arms

In both the North and South, men of all ages were answering the call to action. This is Musician Edwin A. Snyder, who enlisted in Company B of the 2nd Pennsylvania Reserves, which fought alongside Cooper's Battery B in General John Reynolds's Brigade. After the 2nd Regiment's term of service was up, Snyder re-enlisted in Company C of the 191st Pennsylvania Veteran Volunteers – hence the set of Veteran stripes on his sleeves.

CHRONOLOGY
PRIVATE ROBERT DUNNAN'S JOURNEY WITH BATTERY B: 1861 – 1862

1861

April 26:	Organized at Mount Jackson, Lawrence County, Pa.
June 8:	Entered the Pennsylvania State Service.
June 28:	Formally mustered in at Camp Wright, Pennsylvania, near Pittsburgh.
July 23:	Moved by train to Camp Curtin at Harrisburg, Pa.
August 7:	Moved by train to the Arsenal in Washington D.C. and attached to McCall's Pennsylvanian Reserves Division, Army of the Potomac. At Camp Barry, Washington, D.C.
August 14:	At Tenallytown, Maryland, until September.
Sept-Oct:	At Great Falls, Md.
Oct-Dec:	At Camp Pierpont, Langley, Va.
December 20:	McCall's Division saw its first action in the *Battle of Dranesville*, but by the time Battery B arrived the battle was over.
December 25:	Temporarily transferred to Banks's Division. Duty at Seneca Falls and Edward's Ferry on the upper Potomac River.

1862

January 9:	Rejoined McCall's Division, and at Camp Pierpont near Langley until March, 1862.
March-April:	McCall's Pennsylvania Reserves (Second Division) became part of McDowell's 1st Army Corps, Army of the Potomac.
March 10-15:	McDowell advanced on Manassas.
Late March / early April:	At Alexandria awaiting embarkation to the Virginia Peninsula.
April-June:	McCall's Pennsylvania Reserves became part of the Department of the Rappahannock.
April 9-19:	McDowell advanced on Falmouth.

April-June:	Duty at Falmouth and Fredericksburg.
June 13:	Moved down the Rappahannock by boat to White House Landing on the Virginia Peninsula.
June 20:	Joined the Division at Mechanicsville outside Richmond when McCall's Pennsylvania Reserves became the 3rd Division, V Corps, Army of the Potomac.
June 25-July 1:	*Seven Days Battles* before Richmond.
June 26:	*Battle of Beaver Dam Creek (Mechanicsville).*
June 27:	*Battle of Gaines's Mill.*
June 30:	*Battle of Glendale (White Oak Swamp).*
July 1:	*Battle of Malvern Hill.*
July 2:	Arrived at Harrison's Landing.
July 27/29:	Private Dunnan died of disease at Harrison's Landing.

Camp life for the 2nd Pennsylvania Regiment from Reynolds's Brigade

Map opposite page:
Dotted line showing the movements of Private Dunnan and Battery B between August, 1861, and July, 1862, with major locations in bold. Adapted from *Map of the Seat of War* published by T.A. Burke, Savannah. Library of Congress.

BATTERY B

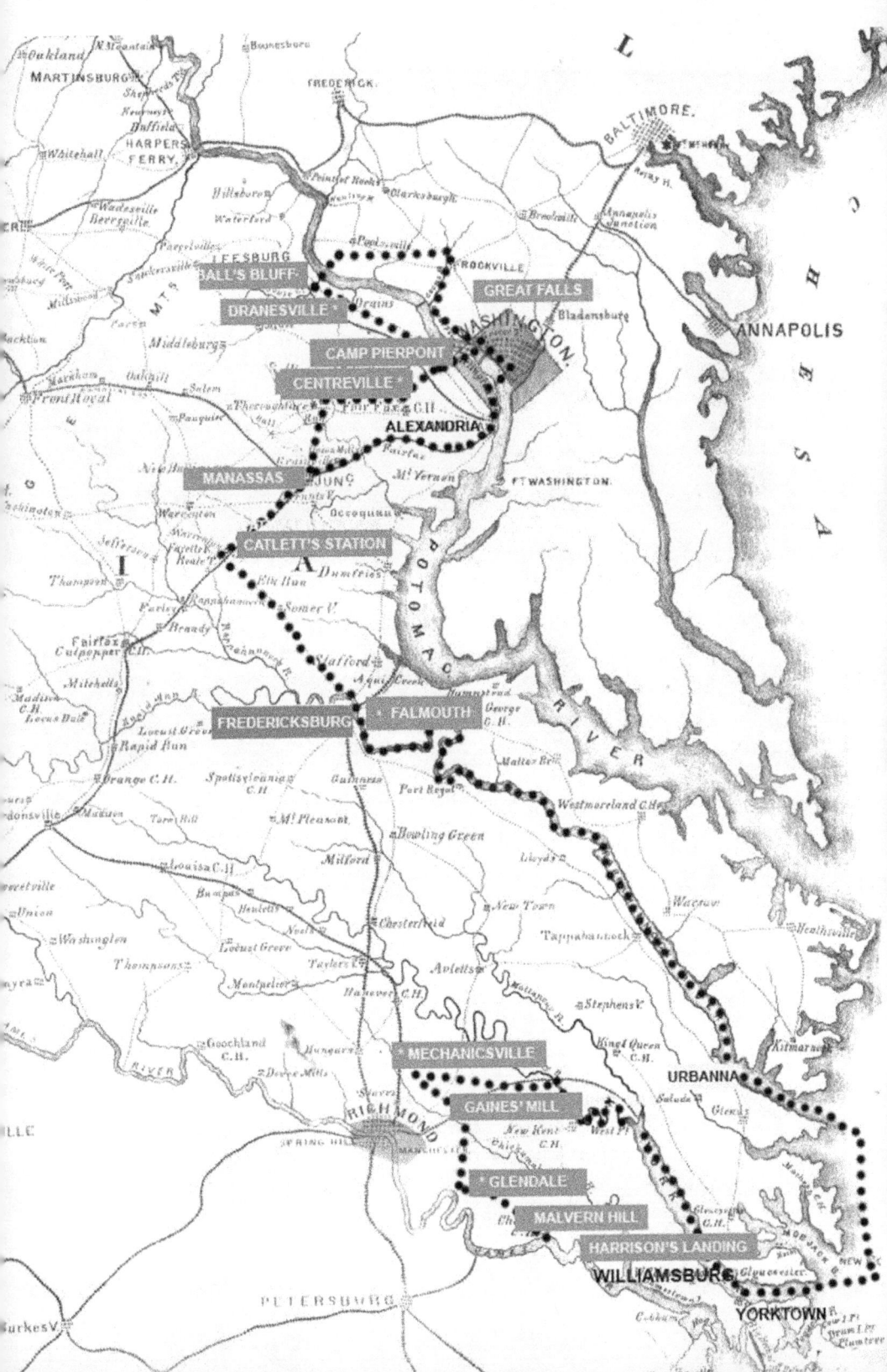

Robert's handwriten entry at front of diary

BATTERY B

The Diary THE STORY

- August 12, 1861

We marched five miles for our horses. it was the pretiest march that we have had since we started from Lawrence. I saw the Presidents house it is a nice building it has Washington's statue in front of it. The united states treasure is a fine building. it is built of marble

- the 13

I was at the united states arsenal it is a nice place. here is the place for to see the big guns and the canon

- the 14

We left Cambell at four a clock for Camp Tannly[6]. it is in the District of Columbia above george town. It is a nice place. we are in camp in the woods and it is covered over with little seaders[7]

Upon its arrival in Washington, the regiment encamped near the Arsenal, where it was more completely armed and equipped, receiving horses for the batteries, and a full supply of ammunition. The batteries then moved to Camp Barry east of the Capitol – named in honor of Major William Barry, at that time the Chief of Artillery.

From Camp Barry the eight batteries were separated and assigned to different divisions, and ultimately, different corps, within the newly established Army of the Potomac, and were never again united as a regiment. Thus it became the first of the 15 Pennsylvania Reserves Regiments to be parted. Batteries A, B, E and G were assigned to General George A McCall's division of Pennsylvania Reserves, in camp at Tenallytown to the north; Battery C to General William F. "Baldy" Smith's Division, in camp near Chain Bridge, Washington; Battery F to General Nathaniel P. Banks's Division, at Poolesville, north of the Potomac River in Maryland; and Batteries D and H to General

---

[6] Camp Tenallytown
[7] Cedars

Don Carlos Buell's Division, in camp north of the city, and engaged in building the fortifications of Washington. This was the Division to which Battery B's Danforth was transferred.

Battery B arrived at Tenallytown on August 14, 1861, and was assigned to the 1st Brigade, commanded by Brigadier General John F. Reynolds, from Lancaster, Pennsylvania.

Guns lined up at the Arsenal in Washington

Camp Tenallytown in 1864

General George McClellan

George Brinton McClellan was a highly regarded graduate from West Point, who first saw action when he served as an engineering officer in the Mexican-American War. He resigned his commission in 1857 to successfully pursue his interests in railroads, and at the outbreak of the Civil War was then much in demand because of the increasing realization that the ability to move troops quickly by rail had the capacity to significantly change the art of warfare. As McClellan wrote, *"It cannot be ignored that the construction of railroads has introduced a new and very important element into war, by the great facilities thus given for concentrating at particular positions large masses of troops from remote sections and by creating new strategic points and lines of operations"*[8]. Indeed many of the battles of the Civil War were fought over railroad junctions.

On May 3, 1861, McClellan was named commander of the Department of the Ohio, responsible for the states of Ohio, Indiana, Illinois, and, later, Western Pennsylvania, Western Virginia, and Missouri. On May 14, he was commissioned a major general in the regular army. Thus at age 34 he outranked everyone in the Army other than Lieutenant General Winfield Scott, by then 74 years old and the Commanding General of the United States Army for the previous 20 years.

McClellan's first battle engagement in the Civil War began with the deployment of his forces to support the people of the northwestern counties of Virginia who felt a strong affinity with the North and objected to the State of Virginia's decision to secede from the Union. McClellan also wanted to keep open the Baltimore and Ohio Railroad line, a critical supply line for the Union.

---

[8] OR, Volume 5, Chapter XIV, p7

McClellan's troops advanced through northwestern Virginia, safeguarding important supply routes as they went. They finally caught the Confederates at an important turnpike at Philippi on June 3, 1861, and launched an attack. The Confederates, who were outnumbered almost four to one, and were poorly armed and poorly trained, turned and fled.

By Civil War standards, the *Battle of Philippi Races* was a minor skirmish – there were 30 casualties in all, four on the Union side and 26 for the Confederates. However it was a Union victory and, for a Northern population short on heroes, it propelled McClellan into public prominence.

McClellan's rapid rise was cemented by the subsequent *Battle of Rich Mountain* which took place on July 11, 1861, in Randolph County, Virginia. In another battle fought over a turnpike, the two-hour engagement and subsequent pursuit of the fleeing Confederates resulted in casualties and losses of 46 Federal troops and 300 Confederates[9]. These actions served to shore up the pro-Union movement within western Virginia and would later lead to the establishment of the State of West Virginia in 1863.

These two minor victories also propelled McClellan to the status of national hero, with the *New York Herald* headlining an article "Gen. McClellan, the Napoleon of the Present War." The day after McDowell led his forces to defeat at the *Battle of Bull Run* on July 21, 1861, Lincoln summoned McClellan to Washington. On July 26, the day he reached the capital, McClellan was appointed commander of the Military Division of the Potomac, the main Union force responsible for the defense of Washington. On August 20, several military units in Virginia were consolidated into his department and McClellan immediately formed the new Army of the Potomac.

Even in the earliest days of his new command, a flaw which would manifest itself throughout McClellan's leadership became evident. On August 8, claiming that the Confederates had more than 100,000 troops facing Washington (in contrast to the 35,000 they actually deployed at Bull Run a few weeks earlier), he declared a state of

---

[9] Casualty figures are often vague, particularly for Confederate forces, but generally include those killed, wounded, missing in action and captured.

emergency in the capital. By August 19, his estimate of the enemy had grown to 150,000.

In fact, in 1861 and 1862 McClellan rarely had less than a two-to-one advantage over the Confederates. Yet time after time, McClellan's war strategy was driven by his belief that his forces were massively outnumbered. The result was a level of extreme caution that often paralyzed any initiative by McClellan's army and led to mounting criticism from within government and the community.

General George McCall

George Archibald McCall was born in Philadelphia, Pa, in 1802 and graduated from West Point in 1822. He served with distinction in a number of engagements, including the Mexican-American War and retired from the army in 1853. As Major General of the state militia at the beginning of the Civil War, McCall helped organize the Pennsylvania volunteers and was commissioned Brigadier General of volunteers in May, 1861. He went on to lead the Pennsylvania Reserves Division, serving as Reserves commander when it operated as the 2nd Division, 1 Corps, Army of the Potomac, and 3rd Division, V Corps. For almost all of his service, Private Robert Dunnan served in McCall's Pennsylvania Reserves Division.

General John Reynolds

John Fulton Reynolds was born in Lancaster, Pa, in 1820 and became one of the Union Army's most respected leaders. He graduated from West Point in 1841 and received high praise (and promotions) for his leadership in various battle arenas including the Mexican-American War. He was the Commandant of Cadets at West Point from September, 1860, to June, 1861, while also serving as an instructor of artillery, cavalry, and infantry tactics. In August, 1861, Reynolds was appointed Brigadier General of the 1st Brigade, Pennsylvania Volunteers. Again, for all but a few days of his service, Private Dunnan served in Reynolds's Brigade (in McCall's Division).

General George A. McCall

General John F. Reynolds

- the 21

We went out on drill and had a grand review. it was nice sean the President Lincoln was out and General McClelland and General McCall. There was a big crowd of spectators out to se us parade

Lincoln was a very hands-on Commander-in-Chief, a style which was not always welcomed by Army officers who saw Army operations and tactics as their responsibility. This led to considerable tension among a number of his commanders about the level of political interference. However his Republican colleagues would not have allowed him as Commander-in-Chief to have operated in any other way. In turn, Army Chief George McClellan was known to cross the line in the other direction – trying to tell Lincoln the politics of doing the job of President and being highly critical of Lincoln privately.

BATTERY B

Troops on parade on Pennsylvania Avenue, Washington

At the outbreak of the war, Washington was a sleepy city of 75,000 people. At the insistence of the southern states, the capital had been established away from the North's major cities on land ceded by the States of Maryland and Virginia – both of them slave-owning states. Even though Maryland remained with the Union as other Southern States seceded, there was considerable antagonism with the North (reflected by protests and even violence against troops travelling from Pennsylvania via train through Baltimore). Washington sat isolated and almost completely unprotected.

On May 23, as soon as word of the secession of the State of Virginia was received, the US Army immediately marched 13,000 troops across the Potomac River into Northern Virginia and began to build up fortifications to protect the main access routes to the capital – the Chain Bridge, Long Bridge, and the Aqueduct Bridge – notably with the establishment of Forts Corcoran and Runyon in what is now Arlington. These were largely wood and earthwork constructions and with the subsequent defeat at Bull Run there was serious concern as to whether the forts could hold back what was seen as a likely imminent attack.

New Army commander General McClellan was appalled by what he saw as the vulnerability of the city and set as his first priority the defense of Washington. This was an area in which McClellan was well equipped: while his reputation for caution would grow quite rapidly, he also had an excellent reputation for administration, organizing and logistics – something which would be enhanced in his time as Army chief.

Even as he set about building up these defenses, which was welcomed by the residents, more broadly in the North there was widespread impatience to see the Army on the front foot against Richmond and the secessionists (a view shared by Lincoln who was keen to see the war ended quickly).

But McClellan also held a deep distrust of the militia, considering that volunteers could not be relied on to perform in battle – a view which he felt was reinforced by the defeat at Bull Run. Therefore a key initial focus for him was to train the volunteers and turn them into a well-equipped, high performing Army – before they were committed to any more battles.

Ultimately 68 forts were erected for the defense of Washington: there is no doubt they acted as a strong deterrent to enemy attack but only one of them ever saw active duty – Fort Stevens, north of the city, in 1864.

> Washington grew rapidly throughout the war as civilians arrived to support both the administration and the army, and by the 1870 census the population had increased to 132,000. The capital also attracted many enslaved people from surrounding areas who first sought sanctuary and protection, and then stayed. The city changed in character from southern origin to northern newcomers and a large African-American population – something which would become a significant factor in the strength of the Civil Rights movement in Washington a century later.

BATTERY B

Washington D.C. barracks and arsenal during the Civil War

- the 26
we left camp tannley for to go to the big fols[10]. we left at eight a clock in the morning and arrived at the fols at three in the afternoon. this is a ruf peas of cuntry. there is now big timber here. it is covert with little pines and sedars and chesnuts. it is ruf land and the rufest roads that i ever saw. the fols is on the petomich twenty miles from Washington. it is the rockiest place that i saw

Battery B marched as part of General McCall's Division to the Great Falls up river from Washington on the northern shore of the Potomac River – the border between Maryland and Virginia.

The Battery remained at the Great Falls until October, as part of the defense around Washington, while the troops were trained and prepared for battle.

---

[10] Falls

Soldiers and civilians at the Great Falls during the Civil War

The Great Falls was seen as one of a number of strategic locations for the defense of Washington as it was close to the intersection of the Georgetown and Leesburg pikes at the small town of Dranesville, as well as the Loudoun and Hampshire Railroad. McClellan was concerned not only about the potential for attack by troops from Virginia crossing the Potomac into Maryland but also the potential for attack from Maryland itself, given widespread hostility to the Lincoln regime. He also feared that if the enemy were able to seize positions in the heights on the Maryland side of the river, they would be able to lob artillery shells into the capital with ease.

BATTERY B

> In many of the entries in his diary, Private Dunnan shows a fascination with the terrain over which he was travelling – a point of familiarity for a young man raised on a farm. And at that time the Great Falls area certainly was rough country – largely bush and wilderness, although it was well mapped because of the work done by the Army Corps of Engineers in planning and commencing construction of the Washington Aqueduct, designed to provide fresh water to the capital.

Diary entry: August 28 AD 1861

Washington Aqueduct
Project by
Capt. Montgomery C. Meigs[11]
U.S. Corps of Engineers
Chief Engineer;
Begun 8th November 1853
By Franklin Pierce President of the U.S
This stone is erected in the unfinished
gate House; at the great falls of the Potomac;
June 10th A.D. 1858
James Buchanan being President of the U.S.
By Capt. M. C. Meigs, Chief Engineer
of the Washington Aqueduct
The assistant Engineers have been W.H. Bryan, C. Crozet, C.G. Talcott, A. L. Rives, W. R. Hutton, E. T. D. Meyers.
Cost of the Work as estimated in 1853 $2,300,000.
Actual cost when finished 18-- $.
Dei Gratia[12]
Esto Perpetua[13]

---

[11] Montgomery C. Meigs, Civil engineer and Quartermaster General of the US Army during and after the War. The aqueduct was completed in 1864 and has been in continuous use ever since in supplying water to Washington D.C.
[12] Latin for "By the Grace of God"
[13] Latin for "Let it be Perpetual"

Washington Aqueduct, which still supplies water to Washington today

The Aqueduct Bridge over the Potomac during the Civil War

- September 1, 1861

I was out at the fawling water. it is a nice senery to see the water rushing down the rocks. I saw sum of the rebles across the river our men fired on them. they run in to the woods. this was the first shooting i saw dun at the rebles. The falls are 20 miles from washington. the rocks split the river into three streams. there is one place where the water falls about 20 feet another 5 & another 15. these falls are within 10 Rods of each other

- the 4

the sesessionists fired on us but did not do any harm to us. we are looking for a tack soon. we sent for reinforcements they comenst firing at half past eight a clock in the morning. Captain Cooper came out with the other batery and to regiments of infantry each one batery of Rhode island artillery. there is three regiments of infantry two companys of artillery and two of cavelry here now.

This was the Pennsylvania Reserves' first real conflict in the war – and in the overall scheme of what was to come it was a very minor skirmish. Battery B's Lieutenant Thomas Cadwalader was on picket with his section at Great Falls when on September 4 Confederate forces fired on the troops guarding that point. The fact that Private Dunnan recorded this in his diary indicates that he was in Lieutenant Cadwalader's section in Battery B – initially the left section but when the Battery went from four to six guns this became the center section.

In his Official Report of September 5, 1861, Pennsylvania Reserves Commander Brigadier General George A. McCall provides the following description: *"I have the honor to report that the enemy having opened fire on the Seventh Infantry of this brigade at Great Falls at 8.30 a.m. yesterday, with two 24-pounder howitzers and three rifle cannon, it was ascertained that our guns did not reach their position (the entrenchment in rear of Dickeys house, already reported), and Colonel Harvey having reported these facts to me, I immediately sent forward two rifle cannon and the Eighth Infantry to support the Seventh, but afterwards recalled the Eighth, as*

> *instructed. At 1 o'clock, however, the Eighth was again put in motion. I afterwards learned that the enemy, after throwing about 50 shells and shot, mostly too high, ceased firing at 11 a.m., which up to 5 p.m. had not been resumed."* [14]

Battery B was first armed with Parrott rifles in October, 1861: they were among the guns Battery B used in the Seven Days Battles.

---

[14] OR, Vol. 5, Ch. XIV, p 127

- *the 7*

the Mt Jackson artillery opened fire across the falls with bum and shot. they fired sixty rounds but the enemy retreated without firing a shot

- *the 25*

we are under marching orders. we are redy for starting. we had the harnis on the horses til the eavening

- *the 26*

we got our pay in gold and silver $12.86 cents

- *the 27*

it is raining here now in the morning

- *the 28*

we got our trowsers in the morning and in the evening we had orders to harnis our horses for to march at a minits warning. the harnis staid on all night

- *the 29*

we got orders to take the harnis of the horsis.

On September 10, at a ceremony attended by President Lincoln and General McClellan and with thousands of troops assembled on parade in Washington, Pennsylvania's Governor Andrew Curtin presented each Regiment with its "colors" – the flags under which and for which they would fiercely and proudly fight throughout the war.

During the summer and fall, McClellan brought a high degree of organization to his new army, and greatly improved its morale by his frequent trips to review and encourage his troops. The circle of forts he had built around Washington were almost impregnable, and the size of the Army of the Potomac grew from 50,000 in July to 168,000 in November – more than twice the size of the civilian population. This was considered a colossal military force.

But it was also a time of tension in the high command, as McClellan continued to quarrel frequently with the government and the General-in-Chief, Lieutenant General Winfield Scott, on matters of strategy. McClellan proposed that his army should be expanded to 273,000 men and 600 guns and "crush the rebels in one campaign."

things are quiet here now. Cowden Rainey was here to day

- the 30

there are a big excitement here today. General McCalls hole bregaid is under arms and the rode is lined with soldiers but they have not got orders to march. J.W. Blanchard was here to day

- October 1, 1861

I drove a team to the slauter house for to get sum meet. while there I saw a beloon across the river in Arlington height. it was pretty high but is did not stay long there. there was a big hail storm here it was the biggest hail that i ever saw

He also openly favored a war that would impose little impact on civilian populations and require no emancipation of slaves – no "taking" of private property.

The first death in the battery was that of Private James M. McClurg which occurred on September 29. McClurg is understood to have died in hospital at Georgetown from disease. His body was buried in the Military Asylum Cemetery in Washington D.C.

The advent of balloons in the Civil War was another example of the transformations occurring in how battles and wars would be fought in the modern world. While relatively minor compared to the impact which aircraft and air forces would bring to warfare, for the first time observation balloons were able to be used to spy on the enemy and gain vital information on their deployment, movements and fortifications.

A key leader in the field of ballooning was Professor Thaddeus S.C. Lowe, who was performing as a showman, giving balloon rides until the advent of the War. Lowe's first military involvement came at the *First Battle of Bull Run*. He performed admirably in sending back information to McDowell about the positioning of Confederate troops. After wind changes forced him to land behind enemy lines, Lowe twisted his ankle and could not escape. But his wife dressed as a hag and drove a covered buckboard past Confederate troops to rescue Lowe and his equipment.

Word of Lowe's exploits got back to the President, who ordered General Winfield Scott to form the Union Army Balloon Corps, with Lowe as Chief Aeronaut, while still remaining a civilian.

Lowe's gas generators being used in the Union Army Balloon Corps

Lowe went on to serve in the Peninsula Campaign of 1862, making observations over Yorktown, as well as at the *Battle of Seven Pines* or *Fair Oaks*, the *Battle of Beaver Dam Creek* or *Mechanicsville*, and the *Battle of Gaines's Mill* (although on that day he was fooled by deliberate Confederate ruses and gave a false impression of the strength of Lee's army south of the Chickahominy River).

At one stage, Lowe was given use of a converted coal barge, the *George Washington Parke Custis*, onto which he loaded two balloons, and then performed the first observations over water – thereby making the *GWP Custis* the first ever aircraft carrier.

> Germany's Count Ferdinand von Zeppelin served as a military observer during the war. Von Zeppelin spent considerable time studying Lowe's aeronautic techniques, both before and after the war, and later designed the dirigible aircraft that bore his name.

- **the 8**
there was a big review of the artillery and cavelry. It was the greatest review that has taken place. The limber box of our cannon blode up near the Presidents house.[15]

- **the 10**
we went to the sity for sum more horses. We got twenty eight

- **the 11**
I was at the US arsenal. we went here for a couple of casons wagons[16]. this is a business place here. now there is four twenty four guns going out now there is a big pile of canon here yet they are cleaning up muskets and preparing everything here for the war. the united states arsenal is situated on the petomick west of Washington Sity on a beautiful peace of ground. the houses are built of brick and has nice shade trees in the park

Until October 11, Battery B was armed with four six-pounder James guns, when two of these were exchanged for four ten-pounder Parrotts. James guns (or James Rifles) were rifled bronze cannon which were in use at the beginning of the war but which could become inaccurate through tube wear and stretching from repeated use.

They were phased out and largely replaced by the newly invented Parrott Rifles. Parrotts were made of cast and wrought iron with banding over the breech to reduce fracturing from repeated firing. The 10-pounders used by Battery B provided for greatly increased accuracy over a much longer range.

By the end of the war, Parrott guns were in widespread use on both sides, although there remained considerable concern about their safety. Prolonged firing would result in the metal becoming brittle resulting in serious risk to the crew that the gun might blow up in their faces. This type of damage would

---

[15] The ammunition box blew up
[16] Caissons – two wheeled carts designed to carry artillery ammunition

occur repeatedly to the guns used by Battery B – the gunners would have to chip out the loosened metal from the breech to be able to keep firing.

Parrott Rifle

- the 12
we got new orders to march. we started at ten a clock in the eavening. it was a nice moon light night. we came across to Virginia. we had sum hard rods to travel. Virginia is a rough rode to travel

- the 13
we have our battery formed in a cornfield. it is a nice looking place here. the land is roling

- the 14
there was a frost this morning the first that i saw here. the third regiment was on dress

Battery B received orders to cross the Potomac with the Division to occupy Langley in Virginia – the present day headquarters of the CIA. The village was located along the Leesburg-Georgetown Turnpike only a few miles from the strategic crossing of the Potomac River at Chain Bridge.

McCall's troops formed the Union front line in Virginia at Camp Pierpont on the land surrounding Langley. Twenty miles away was the Confederate front line at Centreville, and in between were farmlands ripe for foraging troops from both sides.

On October 12, Corporal

parade and one of there guns went of and shot to of our men. there names Phillips and Fred Siphert the later was killed ded

- the 15
Fred Seypherd was sent home. this day is clear and warm

- the 16
we was called out at four a clock for to bee redy for a battle then we got our batry wagon. to day it is cloudy but worm. things is quiet here now but we can hear canons of at a distance up the petomic

- the 18
is clear and worm

James K. M. Bear, one of the original volunteers in the Mt Jackson Guards and from a family which settled in North Beaver Township in 1825, was discharged due to ill health. It was a sign of what was to come.

On October 14, the musket of a member of Company E, 3rd Reserves Regiment, accidentally discharged while on dress parade. Private Frederick B. Seifert, 40, from New Castle, was killed and Private Alfred Phillips, who had enlisted at Harrisburg only three weeks earlier, was discharged in 1862 for wounds received in the accident.

The relationship between McClellan and Winfield Scott as General-in-Chief of the Army deteriorated rapidly. Scott, like many others, was furious that McClellan refused to divulge any details of his plans for the Army of the Potomac. McClellan on the other hand did not trust the administration to keep his plans secret from the press, and thus the enemy. Scott became disillusioned and offered his resignation to President Lincoln. Finally Lincoln's Cabinet met on October 18 and agreed to accept Scott's resignation.

- the 19
we was ordered up at to a clock for to feed our horses. we fed and harnised up and was redy to start at six a clock. we got on the rode heading to leasburgh[17] we was on the rode all day. we stopped in a nice roling field. the country is nice roling land. along the rode we travled it is well timbered. We did not see the enemy but we saw some girls. we got orders to unharnis and feed and we got our supper. after dark the orders came to harnis up. we got on the rode and came back to Draynsville[18]. here we stopped for the night

- the 20
Draynsville has five or six houses in it. it is situated on the rode to leasburgh and the rode to fairfax[19]. it is a nice place for a camp here. it is in Fairfax County. we was in Camden County. it has nice fertal land. we came back to Fairfax County the same day we went out and stopped at Draynsville and lade over there all

Battle of Ball's Bluff
October 21, 1861

On October 19, acting on intelligence that the Confederates may be withdrawing from Leesburg (a Confederate stronghold), McClellan ordered McCall to march his Pennsylvania Reserves Division to nearby Dranesville, to check on Confederate troop movements. At the same time, he ordered Brigadier General Charles Pomeroy Stone to take his Division, which was guarding the crossings in that area along the Upper Potomac, to "keep a good look-out on Leesburg" and to determine whether this show of strength might drive the Confederates off. McClellan suggested that a slight demonstration of force might assist.

McClellan joined McCall that night at Dranesville and then ordered McCall to return his Division to Camp Pierpont at Langley. McCall's troops departed on the morning of October 21 – but Stone was never informed and thought they were always nearby to reinforce him if needed.

After several forays across the Potomac, which made Stone think that the Confederates may indeed

---

[17] Leesburg, Va
[18] Dranesville, Va
[19] Fairfax, Va

day Sunday

- the 21 this morning is cloudy. we got orders to move. we started for camp again. we got back to Camp Pierpont[20] at three a clock. this was a pleasant trip to us but the bois did not like to cum back they would rather went a hed

have been leaving Leesburg, Stone crossed the river at Edward's Ferry into Virginia with part of his Division. He also sent other troops still on the Maryland side of the river further upstream and nearer to Leesburg, to cross to Harrison's Island in the Potomac, and then on to scale the cliffs of Ball's Bluff on the Virginia side of the river.

However the Confederates were waiting east of Leesburg, and their commander, Colonel Nathan G. "Shanks" Evans, sent half of his force to stop Stone near Edward's Ferry, while the remainder was sent to meet the assault via Ball's Bluff.

Finding his way blocked, Stone crossed back to Edward's Ferry and then advanced on the Maryland side of the river towards Harrison's Island, only to find his troops there had been defeated and driven back over the 100 foot cliffs into the river.

Stone then sent for reinforcements from McCall's Division, but they had already left that morning.

Stone lost about 1,000 men killed, wounded, captured, and drowned at Ball's Bluff, while the Confederates lost less than 160. This was the second largest battle of the Eastern Theater in 1861 (after *First Bull Run*)

---

[20] Camp Pierpont, in Langley, Va., north west of Washington, the main quarters of the Pennsylvania Reserves in the winter of 1861-62, and within relatively easy access of the Great Falls area.

and again resulted in a serious defeat of the Union forces.

Very significantly, among those killed was U.S. Senator and Colonel Edward Dickinson Baker, a Republican and long-time close friend of Abraham Lincoln, but with no battle experience. Stone had sent Colonel Baker to Harrison's Island in the river below Ball's Bluff to ensure the safe return of troops who had already crossed the river to reconnoiter and test the strength of the enemy. He gave strict instructions that if the enemy was present in force they should not cross but rather should withdraw those already on the other side.

However, before he had even reached Harrison's Island, Baker ordered hundreds of men to make the difficult crossing and scale the cliffs, with only limited boats in place for any retreat. This resulted in hundreds of men being cut off, killed, captured or drowned, and led to his own death.

Serious political repercussions arose from the defeat (and the Senator's death) and these in particular engulfed General Stone.

General Charles P. Stone and daughter

- the 22
this day is raining we carrede out marching to day

Colonel Charles T. Campbell was the original commander of the 1st Light Artillery Regiment,

– the 23 General Mead and General Ranels[21] and Colonel Campbell tride to of our guns to day to see how they would shoot	Pennsylvania Reserves, although on reaching Washington the various batteries of the regiment were subsequently split across different Divisions. Campbell resigned in February, 1862, and joined the infantry.

General George Meade

George Gordon Meade was born in 1815 and graduated from West Point in 1835. He was a career United States Army officer and civil engineer involved in coastal surveying and construction, including of several lighthouses and breakwaters. He fought with distinction in the Second Seminole War and Mexican-American War.

Meade was promoted from captain to brigadier general of volunteers on August 31, 1861, based on the strong recommendation of Pennsylvania Governor Andrew Curtin. He was assigned command of the 2nd Brigade of McCall's Pennsylvania Reserves.

---

[21] General John F. Reynolds

Troops of the Pennsylvanian Reserves 7th Regiment, from Meade's 2nd Brigade (above and below)

DAVID BUTT

- the 24

this is a nice clear day we are under marching orders to day

- the 28

there was a review of General Ranels devesion. there was five regiments of infantry, five cumpanys of cavelry and three of artillery

- the 29

there was a review of General Ranels and General Mead devesions. there was thirteen regiments of infantry and one of cavelry and three cumpanys of artillery

- the 31

there was a review of artillery and inspection by General Bary. he is a sharp looking oficer

General William F. Barry, first Chief of Artillery under Major General McClellan

- *Nov 1, 1861*

I went out to Comodor Toll Jones old residence. It is a nice place. W McGines came here to day[22]

- *the 2*

it rained here all day and everything is wett now

- *the 16*

we got our pay to day

- *the 22*

there was a shote battle fot in General Smith's Devesion[23]

- *the 23*

this day was clear and cold

On November 1, 1861, Winfield Scott retired and McClellan became General-in-Chief of all the Union armies. President Lincoln raised his concerns about the *"vast labor"* involved in the dual role of Army Commander and General-in-Chief, but McClellan responded, *"I can do it all."*

However the rout at Ball's Bluff had left McClellan with the firm conviction that his troops were not ready for battle. November passed, winter arrived and the combination of the weather and the state of the roads made a major engagement virtually impossible. As frustrated as many in the North may have been because of this lack of progress, there would be no move against the Confederates before Spring.

---

[22] W. McGines is thought to be William McGinnis, the father of one or more of the four McGinnises who joined Battery B from Western Pennsylvania that year – Samuel (an original Mt Jackson recruit who was wounded at *Second Bull Run* on August 29, 1862, and later promoted to Sergeant), James and George (both were mustered in at Harrisburg on September 11 – James died from disease on May 24, 1862), and Alvin (mustered in at Harrisburg on October 6 and discharged for medical reasons on February 3, 1862).

[23] Brigadier General William "Baldy" Smith, commander of the 2nd Division. Smith's Division would initially form part of the IV Corps of the Army of the Potomac at the start of the Peninsula Campaign, but would move to VI Corps under Brigadier General William B. Franklin when it was formed just prior to the *Seven Days Battles*.

- **the 24**
I was on guard. There was a heavy frost this morning and in the evening there was snow

- **the 27**
there was a big excitement in camp. There was twelve sesesh taken prisoners the first that I have seen

- **Dec the 3, 1861**
we got orders for to march in the morning. We stated for Draynesville we got within six miles

Two pages impossible to read
...three cumpanys of artillery and one regiment of cavalry

- **the 17**
there are eight …..came…..to our …..late in the evening there was ten rebles guerillas taken by our pickets. One of them was Captain Kern[24]

The "sesesh" referred to by Private Dunnan were probably local farmers and townspeople. The area between the Union front line at Langley and the Confederate front line at Centreville and Leesburg was predominately occupied by supporters of the South (after all, it was Northern Virginia), and the Union forces were not averse to arresting those they thought were potential spies or trouble-makers.

On December 18, Private John W. Runshaw was discharged because of ill health.

---

[24] Battery G commander, Captain Mark Kern

- *the 20* at an early hour General ----- bregaid ----- the first regiment of rifles and Easton[25] batery four pieces of canon

----

----
reconnoitring expedition towards Drainsville half way between town Leasburgh -------- at ------------ at Drainsville they encountered the rebles who had four regiments of infantry one of cavelry and one batery of artillery. the engagement lasted one hour and a half.

General Ranels left camp at eight a clock and went in the rear and formed on the left. he hird firing to the right of him he ordered his men forward when orders came to him for him to cum up in the rear

Battle of Dranesville
December 20, 1861

By Civil War standards this was a relatively small engagement. However, the *Battle of Dranesville* was significant for the Pennsylvania Reserves because it was their first real battle. Very importantly, it also was the first time in the East that the Union Army had triumphed over the Confederates.

The battle took place between Confederate forces under General J.E.B. Stuart and the 3rd Brigade of the Pennsylvania Reserves under General Edward O.C. Ord (Reynolds and Meade commanded the 1st and 2nd brigades respectively). This was not a planned attack by either side: the two forces were out foraging and patrolling as winter was setting in when they met and engaged one another for two hours at the crossroads at Dranesville.

Battery A of the 1st Light Artillery of the Pennsylvania Reserves had been recruited at Chambersburg, Franklin County, and was under the command of Captain Hezekiah Easton, in General Ord's Brigade. Battery A thereby became the first battery from the Pennsylvania Reserves to be engaged in anything more than a skirmish and distinguished itself by knocking out the Confederate guns. However their success also owed much to the actions of General Ord, an experienced

---

[25] Battery A commander Captain Hezekiah Easton

> **which he did in double quick to the battle ground to late for the battle was over**

artilleryman, who spent considerable time positioning their guns and directing their fire.

The Union Army then drove back the Confederates and pursued them for a half mile before breaking off and heading back towards Langley.

General McCall later described[26] how he had ridden up to Easton's Battery when it was *"in full blast upon the enemy's battery, about 500 yards in front of the Centreville road....while here, admiring the beautiful accuracy of the shot and shell thrown by this battery upon the battery of the enemy, a force of infantry and cavalry made their appearance from cover....but a few shell from our battery skillfully thrown into their midst checked their advance and drove them back ignominiously to cover."*

When they had reached the position where the enemy's battery had been placed, McCall recounted *"and here we had evidence of the fine artillery practice of Easton's Battery. The road was strewn with men and horses; two caissons, one of them blown up; a limber; a gun-carriage wheel; a quantity of artillery ammunition, small-arms, and an immense quantity of heavy clothing, blankets, etc."*

Captain Hezekiah Easton wrote that *"the woods in which the enemy were concealed were found thickly strewn with dead and wounded. The mangled bodies of the dead showed the terrible execution of*

---

[26] OR, Vol. V, Ch. XIV, pp. 474-475

our fire....*although the injury and loss of the enemy was so severe, in my battery there was not a man or horse lost and no injury done my guns. Our only casualty was the slight wounding of one of my men (Charles Osborn), who was struck in the knee by a spent ball, which slightly lamed him."*

Battery B was with Reynolds's 1st Brigade at Difficult Creek, two miles from the front, ready to support Ord if needed. When Reynolds heard the sound of the artillery, he moved his troops forward rapidly but by the time he arrived the battle was over. Meade also had heard gunfire and began moving his brigade forward. As McCall pointed out, Ord's brigade *"had left nothing for Reynolds and Meade to do."*

There were 71 Union casualties, and 230 among the Confederates.

General Edward Ord and family

> The *Battle of Dranesville* was that rarest of things in the Eastern Zone in 1861 – a Union victory. In fact, it was such good news for the North that Secretary of War Simon Cameron took the unusual step of writing a letter of commendation to McCall: *"I cannot refrain from expressing to you my admiration of the gallant conduct displayed by both officers and men in this their first contest with the enemy… I feel that I have just cause to be proud that, animated by no other motive than patriotism, they are among the first to revive the glory shed upon our country by the men of the Revolution and the soldiers of the war of 1812. It is one of the bright spots that give assurance of the success of coming events, and its effect must be to inspire confidence in the belief that hereafter, as heretofore, the cause of our country will triumph. I am especially gratified that a Pennsylvania artillery corps, commanded by officers who have necessarily had but limited systematic instruction, have won not only the commendation of their friends, but an unwilling compliment from the enemy for the wonderful rapidity and accuracy of their fire….Other portions of the Army will be stimulated by their brave deeds, and men will be proud to say that at Dranesville they served under McCall and Ord."* OR, Volume V, Chapter XIV, p 477.

- the 25

this is Christmas here and the driest day that i have seen here. we got marching orders to day for to go and join General Stones devesion

On December 25, General McClellan, in compliance with a request from General Banks for a "good battery" to join his Division on the upper Potomac, directed General McCall to send Battery B. This was protested against by Generals McCall and Reynolds, and caused much dissatisfaction throughout the Division.

- *the 26*
we took our line of march at Camp Pierpont and crossed the chain bridge passed thru Georgetown and stopped at camp tennly. here we eat our dinner and then started on the rode for Rockville the county seat of Montgomery county, here we staid all night in the fair ground it is a nice place for to stay here everything is convenient here

General Stone's forces, which had been involved in the defeat at Ball's Bluff near Edward's Ferry in October, were headquartered at Poolesville with Banks's Division, and with troops stationed at various crossings along the river.

Battery B was then put on duty at Seneca Falls and Edward's Ferry on the Potomac.

The Chain Bridge during the Civil War connecting Washington D.C. with Arlington and Fairfax Counties in Virginia.

- the 27

we left Rockville in the morning and passed through Darnstown[27]. this is a small town. We went on to Brockville and from that to Poolesville. This is a nice Town. here is where General Stone has his hed quarters. We stopped in camp "Wilks"[28] and staid here for the night.

- the 28

we got orders for to go to Edwards fery

- the 29

we started for Edwards fery it is four miles from Poolesville. This is a nice place for to camp. we have a good view a cross the river and up the River to Bolls Bluff[29]

- the 30

we were set at cleaning our harnis for inspection

- the 31

we were mustred in for our pay to day

On December 27, Private John T. Penrod, one of the original Mt Jackson Guard recruits, was discharged due to ill health. Winter was taking its toll.

---

[27] Darnstown, Montgomery County, Md.
[28] Camp Wilkes at Poolesville, Md., a few miles from Edward's Ferry and Ball's Bluff on the Potomac River.
[29] Ball's Bluff, Loudoun County, Va.

Joint Committee on the Conduct of the War

President Lincoln, along with many other leaders and citizens of the North, became increasingly impatient with McClellan's reticence to attack the Confederate forces still massed in front of Washington. Spurred on by the loss at Ball's Bluff and the death of Colonel and Republican Senator Baker, in December, the Congress formed a *Joint Committee on the Conduct of the War*. The Joint Committee's particular focus was on the loyalty and performance of officers (particularly Democrats), and it became a thorn in the side of many throughout the war, accusing them of incompetence and, in some cases, treason.

McClellan was called as the first witness on December 23, but he contracted typhoid fever and could not attend. Instead, his subordinate officers testified, and their frank admissions that they had no knowledge of specific strategies for advancing against the Confederates raised many calls for McClellan's dismissal.

McClellan was spared but Brigadier General Charles Stone, the divisional commander at the *Battle of Ball's Bluff*, was not as fortunate. Even though there was evidence that Senator Baker had made numerous mistakes in leading the troops at Ball's Bluff which resulted in his death and that of many others, the Republicans laid the blame  with Stone, who was a highly experienced combat officer but was also known as a Democrat. Stone was arrested on February 8, 1862, and jailed for six months – no charges were ever filed and nor did he ever stand trial, which was totally contrary to military law at the time.

Stone was at first kept in solitary confinement in a military prison otherwise used for secessionists. When his health began to fail, he was transferred to another military prison. He was finally released on August 16, 1862, and in 1863 General Stone was exonerated of any fault.

With the facts now known, the New York Times stated in an editorial: *"General Stone has sustained a most flagrant wrong—a wrong which will probably stand as the very worst blot on the National side in the history of the war."*

Stone was never again given a senior position in the Army in the Civil War and finally resigned in September, 1864.

Famed War artist Alfred R. Waud's depiction of how bodies were being pulled out of the Potomac down river from Ball's Bluff for days afterwards.

- Jan 1, 1862

we started puting up stabling for our horses

- the 8

we got orders for to go back to camp Pierpont

- the 10

we took up our line of march back for old Virginia. it was fogy all day and the ride was mudy. we got to rockville at night

- the 11

we left Rockville in the morning and came thru Tenly town. This was a nice day to travel there was a pig fawled us from Tenly across the Chain Bridges to our camp. There was a review of General McCall Devesion to day

- the 19

George Cooper and George Bender came here to day.[30] It is raining here to day and cold and mudy

---

On January 9, at General McCall's request, Battery B was ordered to return to McCall's Division at Camp Pierpont, Langley, Va.

On January 10, President Lincoln met with a number of the top generals without McClellan present and directed them to formulate a plan of attack, stating: *"If General McClellan does not want to use the army, I would like to borrow it for a time."*

Two days later, McClellan was summoned to the White House, where the Cabinet demanded to hear his war plans. For the first time, he revealed his intentions to transport the Army of the Potomac by ship to Urbanna, Virginia, a small town on the Rappahannock River.

Northern Virginia is split by a series of rivers which flow roughly from west to east into Chesapeake Bay. The furthest north is the Potomac, which also forms the border between Virginia and Maryland. Heading progressively south, the rivers are the Rappahannock, then the York, and then the James. These rivers

---

[30] These visitors are thought to be George Cooper, father of Captain James Cooper, and George Bender, father of Private George Bender, another of the original recruits from Mt Jackson. Private George Bender was wounded at *Second Bull Run* on August 29, 1862.

- **the 24**

in the eavening it rained and sleated all night I was on guard

- **the 27**

the day is warm and we got paid for two months $26.02c

Secretary of War Edwin Stanton who replaced Simon Cameron in January, 1862

in turn split the east of the State into a series of peninsulas or necks. Again from north to south these are the Northern Neck (bounded by the Potomac and the Rappahannock), Middle Peninsula (Rappahannock and York), and Virginia Peninsula or Southern Neck (York and James). Further inland, where the rivers were narrower and bridges could be built, were the roads and railways which ran between Washington, Richmond and the surrounding areas. It was on and around these vital junctions that the Confederates had established strong positions at Leesburg, Manassas, Centreville and Fredericksburg – all within easy reach of Washington.

McClellan's Urbanna plan involved bypassing the Confederate forces by sailing down Chesapeake Bay and up the Rappahannock River to Urbanna, on the river's southern shore and the north shore of the Middle Peninsula. This would place a large Union army behind General Joseph E. Johnston's Confederate forces near Washington, with McClellan's plan to then march 50 miles overland to capture Richmond. However because of his concerns about security he refused to give any specific details of the proposed campaign, even to newly appointed Secretary of War, Edwin M. Stanton, a Democrat and – at that time – friend of McClellan.

Lincoln was not convinced but rather favored more direct action against Johnston's forces, to drive them away from Washington. But most of all he desired some form of action, as did an impatient public.

On January 27, Lincoln issued an order that required all of his armies to begin offensive operations by February 22, Washington's birthday.

On January 31, Lincoln issued a supplementary order for the Army of the Potomac to move overland to attack the Confederates at Manassas Junction and Centreville. McClellan quickly replied with a 22-page letter objecting in detail to the President's plan and advocating instead his Urbanna plan which would *"save time, money and lives"*. Although Lincoln preferred his own plan, he was relieved that McClellan finally had committed to action, and reluctantly agreed.

- February 1, 1862 there was two inches of Snow on the ground this morning and it rained thru the Day. James Smith came here to day *- the 15* it snode all day and I went up to the hospital and got vexinated	In early February, three more soldiers – Privates A.H. Germer, Alvin G. McGinnis and John N. Weir – were discharged from the Battery due to illness. This was probably a smallpox vaccination.

"The medicine practiced in Virginia by the Union and Confederate armies during the American Civil War was state of the art for its day and an important factor in the ability of both governments to raise and maintain armies in the field. More than twice as many soldiers died of disease than from combat-related injuries. Still, despite many nineteenth-century misconceptions about the causes and treatments of disease, three out of four soldiers survived their illnesses. This was due in part to widespread vaccination for smallpox, isolation of most contagious diseases, and especially the recognition of the importance of cleanliness and sanitation.

As the war dragged on, combat injuries became more prevalent and the work of surgeons became more important. Surgery, though unsterile, saved lives through amputation. Such procedures were done, for the most part, with adequate pain control and some form of anesthesia.

To care for the wounded, both sides established a system of hospitals, ranging from makeshift field hospitals and interim "corps hospitals" (used by Confederates), to large, fixed general hospitals such as the sprawling Chimborazo Hospital in Richmond. It was often painful and dangerous for the wounded to be transported from the battlefield to the hospital, but in the end the quality of medical care they received was generally high and led to important medical advances during the postwar period and twentieth century."[31]

---

[31] From *Medicine in Virginia During the Civil War*, by T. A. Wheat
http://encyclopediavirginia.org/Medicine_in_Virginia_During_the_Civil_War

- **the 16**

I took a walk to a farm house it was the first house that i have been in since i came here

- **the 23**

we fired a seloot in memory of General Washington birth day

- **the 25**

Mrs Fullerton and Mrs Officer came here to sea the rifol ----[32]

- **the 26**

No. 3 and four went to Washington citty to exchange guns. we got two twelve pown hortzers

- **the 27**

the section No. one and three went out to fier at a target. we got orders to hold ourselves in rediness to march

It is often forgotten that in war soldiers were not sheltered in houses or comfortable barracks. In spring, summer and autumn, when armies would often be on the move, their main shelter was their canvas tents. In winter they would build split log huts, usually with earthen floors, and live closely together in confined spaces where diseases were easily spread.

Howitzers were smoothbore (un-rifled) short-barreled guns that were designed to fire explosive shells in a high trajectory, over a shorter range than rifled guns. They also were effective for close range fighting, using spherical case shot and canister for firing at enemy forces advancing in the open. Howitzers were considered the weapon of choice if the opposing forces were concealed behind hills, forests or fortifications as they could lob projectiles over the top from up high.

---

[32] Mrs. Fullerton and Mrs. Officer are likely to be the mothers of four members of the Battery: the three Fullerton brothers – James, John and Walt – and William Officer, all of whom were original recruits from Mt Jackson. First Lieutenant James Fullerton and Sergeant Walter Fullerton were both discharged due to ill health on December 7, 1862. First Sergeant John M. Fullerton and Corporal William Officer served their full terms.

Captured Howitzer and Union troops

- *March 1, 1862*
it was clear and cold and high winds

While Lincoln had accepted McClellan's Urbanna plan, it was now spring, the roads would soon become passable again, and still there was no sign of action.

Lincoln's deadline of Washington's Birthday to begin the offensive against the Confederates had passed and McClellan was still getting his army ready. McClellan had received some reprieve in pressure from the President for action by that date due to the death from typhoid of Lincoln's third son, Willie, aged 11, at the White House on February 10 – probably caused by the unsanitary nature of the drinking water from the Potomac due to the large numbers of troops camped along its banks.

However despite that tragedy the war needed to be won. The Congress

	and the public were becoming increasingly frustrated with McClellan's lack of progress, and Lincoln remained pessimistic about the proposed Peninsula Campaign.
- the 2 it is snowing to day. General McColl and General Biddle was here to day	"General" Biddle was probably Captain Henry Jonathan Biddle, Assistant Adjutant-General on General McCall's staff. Biddle, a graduate of West Point in 1835, was shot at the *Battle of Glendale* on June 30, 1862. When McClellan's army withdrew, many of the seriously wounded were left behind. Biddle was captured and died of his wounds in Chimborazo Hospital, the main Confederate hospital in Richmond, on July 20. McCall was by his side when he died.

At the time of the formation of the Army of the Potomac, it was initially made up of a small number of Divisions. But as more troops and regiments had flooded into Washington, the number of Divisions had grown and the structure was becoming somewhat unwieldy.

On March 8, with still no sign of action from McClellan, Lincoln called together all 12 of McClellan's Divisional commanders and had them vote on the merits of the Urbanna plan. The Generals voted in favor of the plan 8-4. Lincoln then took the highly unusual step of announcing the formation of four infantry corps, with each assigned a small number of Divisions, as well as the four corps commanders who would answer to McClellan in the Peninsula campaign – this without consulting McClellan, who had been reluctant to name his commanders until he had seen them in action in the field (even though, from a military perspective, it would have been suicidal to have gone into battle without any clear chain of command).

The four named were:
- 1 Corps' Brigadier General Irvin McDowell
- II Corps' Brigadier General Edwin V Sumner
- III Corps' Brigadier General Samuel P. Heintzelman
- IV Corps' Brigadier General Erasmus D. Keyes

I Corps' McDowell

II Corps' Sumner

III Corps' Heintzelman

IV Corps' Keyes

McCall's Pennsylvania Reserves Division was assigned to I Corps under McDowell, with Generals Reynolds, Meade and Truman Seymour as Brigade commanders and Batteries A, B and G of the 1st Pennsylvania Light Artillery, along with Battery C of the 5th US Light Artillery, forming the Division artillery.

General Truman Seymour

While those four Corps were to be led by McClellan in the attack on Richmond, at Lincoln's insistence, a fifth corps – that of General Nathaniel Banks – was to remain behind to defend Washington.

But even as this was occurring, McClellan's Urbanna plan was unraveling. In February, the Confederates decided they were overextended and would withdraw from Manassas and Centreville to positions closer to Richmond. Manassas was well supplied and well equipped, including with heavy artillery, and the Confederates wanted to save as much of those supplies as possible, and certainly did not want to leave any of it behind for the Union Army.

Confederate Commander General Joseph E. Johnston began removing the supplies as quickly as possible along the single-track Orange and Alexandria Railroad. Then, in early March, Johnston noticed increased Union activity in the area. Concerned that an attack might be imminent and his troops might be outflanked, he ordered an immediate withdrawal, and directed his troops to destroy whatever they could not carry with them.

In fact, the Union Army only became aware of the Confederate withdrawal when they spotted the smoke of burning supply depots. But by the time they arrived the Confederates were gone. Johnston relocated his army south of the Rappahannock, meaning that any Union Army landing at Urbanna would still have Johnston's forces between them and Richmond. Urbanna was now off the agenda.

Confederate General
Joseph E. Johnston

McClellan revised his strategy, planning instead to sail further south down Chesapeake Bay, bypass the Middle Peninsula, and land at Fort Monroe, at the bottom of the Virginia Peninsula, which was still a Union stronghold. From there he proposed that they march up the peninsula, with support provided by gunboats and transports using the York and James Rivers, and converge on Richmond.

On March 8 – the same day the Union army realized Manassas and Centreville had been evacuated – McClellan's plans were dealt a further blow when the *CSS Virginia*, the world's first ironclad warship, suddenly appeared and wreaked havoc on the Union's wooden warships anchored in Hampton Roads, off Fort Monroe. The easy success of the *Virginia* had Washington spooked about the wisdom of McClellan's plan to transport troops by ship, and any use of naval support operations on the James River seemed fraught with danger. There also was serious concern about the potential risk of the *CSS Virginia* travelling up the Potomac and launching an attack on Washington. Fortunately, the first US Navy ironclad, the *USS Monitor*, arrived in Hampton Roads the very next day, engaged the *Virginia*, and the two prototype battleships fought to a draw, thus quickly rebalancing the US Navy power.

McClellan came in for further criticism when it was realized that Johnston's forces had not only slipped away unnoticed, but had fooled the Union Army through the use of logs painted black to appear as cannons, nicknamed Quaker Guns. The Congress's joint committee visited the abandoned Confederate lines and a resolution demanding the dismissal of McClellan was only narrowly defeated.

Quaker guns at the abandoned Confederate Fort at Centreville

Lincoln had finally had enough. On March 11, 1862, he removed McClellan as General-in-Chief of all his armies, leaving him in command of only the Army of the Potomac. McClellan was at Manassas when he received notification by telegram, advising that the decision had been made to enable him to devote all his attention to the move on Richmond. But the position of General-in-Chief was not immediately filled by another officer: rather, Lincoln, Stanton, and a group of officers called the "War Board" directed the strategic actions of the Union armies that spring.

In practice, this often meant that day-to-day command was managed by Lincoln and Stanton, or indeed largely Lincoln. He would spend an increasing number of hours in the quiet of the cipher room in the Department of War building, next to the White House, communicating with his generals and other officers to track what was going on at the battle front, and chatting with the cipher decoders in the long periods spent waiting for news.

Union forces occupy abandoned Confederate defenses at Manassas

- the 10

the grand army moved on the Petomac. we moved out to Louden and Hampshire Railrode[33] the first day

- the 11

we moved out and took our position where the rebles was on the q. it is hard country out here

- the 12

we did not make any move to day

On March 10, McDowell's I Corps advanced to Manassas and Centreville, confirming that the Confederates had departed, and had tried to destroy all that they had been forced to leave behind.

The Federals took over the fortified positions previously occupied by the Confederates, and then, on March 15, McDowell's I Corps returned to Alexandria, with McClellan leaving a part of Banks's command at Manassas and Centreville. McClellan's plan was to take McDowell's 1 Corps with him to the Peninsula, believing that Banks's Corps would meet

---

[33] Loudoun and Hampshire Railroad, which ran from Leesburg along the Potomac to Alexandria

- **the 13**

it rained sum and Milton Nesbit came out to see us[34]

- **the 14**

we left camp at night to go back to the pike road

- **the 15**

we started in the morning and went all day it rained on us the half of the time we stopped in the woods and built on a big fire to warm at

- **the 17**

we got on the rode near to Alexandria where we are laying now

- **March the 22**

There was a grand review of General McDowl core Devesion. it was the biggest review that i have seen yet

- **the 27**

I was at the citty of Washington

Lincoln's requirement that McClellan must leave the capital *"entirely secure"*.

McClellan's Army began to sail from Alexandria on March 17. It was an armada that exceeded all previous American expeditions, transporting 121,500 men, 44 artillery batteries, 1,150 wagons, more than 15,000 horses, and tons of equipment and supplies.

Battery B was at Alexandria with McDowell's I Corps awaiting their turn to embark. But progress was slow. The civilian transports of steamers, sloops, ferryboats, canal boats and barges, supported by naval vessels, had to make repeated journeys back and forth, sometimes in heavy weather, and then go through the processes of disembarking men, animals, supplies, wagons, artillery and other equipment.

Ultimately it took about 20 days to move the entire army. But by the time it was coming around to Battery B's turn to embark for the Peninsula, the plans were unraveling again.

---

[34] Milton Nesbit is likely to be the father of the Nesbit brothers, original recruits from Mt Jackson – First Lieutenant Isaac A. Nesbit, who was dismissed on March 14, 1864, and Sergeant James T. Nesbit who was wounded at Mechanicsville on June 26, 1862, and again at Fredericksburg on December 13, 1862.

THE VALLEY CAMPAIGN: PART 1

With I Corps preparing to embark for the Peninsula with II, III and IV Corps, Banks's Corps had been assigned responsibility for the defense of Washington, and had taken over the fortifications at Manassas and Centreville. Banks also moved south of the Potomac River into the Shenandoah Valley to the west of the Manassas plains, and bounded by the Blue Ridge Mountains on one side and the Allegheny Mountains on the other, to guard key road and rail links for the north.

Stonewall Jackson commanded the Confederate forces in the Valley and, when the Confederates withdrew from Manassas, Jackson withdrew from his headquarters at Winchester, which was then occupied by Banks's troops.

With the Valley supposedly secured, Banks began to return some of his troops to Washington, to free up other troops to join McClellan on the Peninsula. But the Confederates had other ideas and General Johnston ordered Jackson to prevent Banks from leaving the Valley, and to divert as many Federals as possible away from Richmond.

Jackson's first battle in the Valley Campaign was at Kernstown on March 23 and resulted in a Union victory – Jackson's only loss of the war. But it more than served its purpose because Lincoln became so alarmed that he immediately ordered Banks back to the Valley and detached 10,000 troops from Sumner's II Corps - a part of McClellan's forces – to support Major General John C. Frémont's Mountain Department in western Virginia. Lincoln also began to seriously reconsider whether even more troops were required to defend Washington.

On April 4, McClellan ordered most of his forces at Fort Monroe on the Virginia Peninsula to move out towards Yorktown. He also wrote to McDowell to advise where I Corps should disembark on the York River on its arrival.

The following day, McClellan was stunned to receive news that the President had decided to withhold McDowell's I Corps for the defense of Washington:

"The President, deeming the force to be left in front of Washington insufficient to insure its safety, has directed that McDowell's army corps

should be detached from the forces operating under your immediate direction. Major-General McDowell has accordingly been instructed to report for orders to the Secretary of War."[35]

McClellan was in disbelief. With 37,000 men, I Corps – now renamed the Department of the Rappahannock – was the largest in the Army. When combined with Lincoln's decision to send 10,000 troops to Frémont in western Virginia in case Stonewall Jackson headed in that direction, it reduced McClellan's army by almost 50,000. This became a further important factor in McClellan's cautious approach throughout the Peninsula Campaign.

McClellan protested and asked Lincoln to change his mind, or to at least let one of McDowell's Divisions – that led by Brigadier General William B. Franklin – join his command. Secretary of War Stanton responded confirming that Franklin's Division would march to Alexandria to embark (Franklin became Commander of a new VI Corps) and that McCall's Pennsylvania Reserves would be detached from McDowell's troops and sent *"if the safety of this city will permit"*.

- *April 10, 1862* **We left Alexandria and came to Centreville. we staid here all night in the Rebles quarters. they had a nice place for to stay and they had it well fortified and brest works thode up[36]. it would have been hard for to take if they had made a stand**	As the main Army of the Potomac was working its way up the Peninsula, Battery B turned around and marched away from the departure port of Alexandria toward Centreville and Manassas, and the defense of other vital positions between Washington and Richmond. From Manassas, Battery B ventured further south with the Union forces, crossing Bull Run

---

[35] OR, Vol. 11, Part 3 p.67

[36] "Breast works thrown up". Breast works are barriers built to protect batteries and troops from attack – usually mounds of earth and/or logs backed by ditches and often with extra obstacles to the front.

DAVID BUTT

- the 11

we left Centreville in the morning for Manassa Junction. we went over sum of the rufest rods to we got to Bulls run. here we are on the plain of Manassa. It is a beautiful place for to look over the Blu Ridge Mountains running south on one side which gives a nice senery

- April the 18

we left Manassa Junction for to go south ward. we travled thru sum nice country. it is level and well watered. we arrived at Catletts Station. there is but one or two houses here. this would bee a good place for a villedge. it is the best farming land that I have saw in Virginia

and moving parallel to the Orange and Alexandria Railroad on the road to Culpeper through which Johnston had withdrawn with his forces.

Only four days earlier, on the open, rolling farmlands near Catlett's Station, General George Stoneman's cavalry and accompanying infantry forces had caught up with the rearguard of Johnston's retreating troops.

An assault on the Confederates was led by two young officers, Lieutenants George Armstrong Custer and John B. McIntosh. Seeing the size of the force pursuing them, the Confederates retreated, burning the bridge crossing Cedar Run and preventing an immediate pursuit.

Four months later, on August 22, in the days leading up to *Second Bull Run*, Confederate Cavalry Commander General J. E. B. Stuart raided Union General John Pope's headquarters at Catlett's Station. Unable to burn the railroad bridge because of a heavy thunderstorm, Stuart withdrew his troops as well as 300 Federal prisoners, Pope's orders and dispatches, a huge store of Federal supplies, and General Pope's hat, cloak and frock coat - which were sent back to Richmond for public display as war trophies.

- the 20

It rained all day and it is cold

- the 29

it rained to day and the bois had a Dog fight[37]

- May 1, 1862

we left Catletts Station and crossed Seder cree

- the 2

we have harnised up redy to start in the morning. we staid on the farm of Mrs Hill. we traveled nineteen miles to day. we stopped in camp near Falmouth

- the 23

the Pennsylvania Reserve was Reviewed by President Lincoln and Edwart M Stanton Secretary of War

Between April 9 and 19, McDowell's troops advanced on Falmouth, on the north side of the Rappahannock River, opposite Fredericksburg, to discover that the Confederates had withdrawn from the town towards Richmond. On April 21, Lincoln wrote to McClellan and advised:

"Your dispatch of the 19th was received that day. Fredericksburg is evacuated and the bridges destroyed by the enemy, and a small part of McDowell's command occupies this side of the Rappahannock, opposite the town. He purposes moving his whole force to that point."[38]

Throughout April, the Valley Campaign involved a series of moves and counter moves from both sides, with Jackson generally retreating south (up the Valley) before Banks to find more favorable positions and with no really decisive battles. With the Valley

---

[37] Dog fighting became popular entertainment in the 1860s with dogs being imported from England and Ireland shortly before the Civil War.
[38] OR, Vol 11, Part 3, p 117

supposedly under control, plans were then hatched for McDowell to press on overland towards Richmond, with the aim of McDowell attacking from the north at the same time as McClellan was attacking from the east.

Sending McCall's Division by water to reinforce McClellan also was still under consideration However it was recognized this would severely weaken McDowell's ability to push on overland to Richmond. So in late April, Lincoln decided to detach Brigadier General James Shields's division from Banks's Corps and transfer it to McDowell at Fredericksburg. This left Banks in the Valley with only a single division to guard against Jackson. Banks was then instructed to retreat down the valley and establish a defensive position at Strasburg in the north.

General "Stonewall" Jackson was a graduate of West Point Academy in the same class as General George McClellan.

While Battery B had so far escaped the hardships of the swamps of the Peninsula, it was still severely hit by disease even as it served near Washington. In May, four members of the battery died: Private Robert Chambers died on May 4, Private Hernando J. Duff on May 7, Private James McGinnis on May 24, and Private Charles B. Elwell on May 31. Chambers and Duff were original members of the Mt Jackson Guards. Three other Battery members – Private David W. Frew, Artificer Theodore McWilliams and Private John C. Hughston – were discharged due to illness. Hughston subsequently recovered and reenlisted in the Battery but later died from disease.

THE PENINSULA CAMPAIGN: PART 1
Advance on Yorktown and the **Battle of Williamsburg**

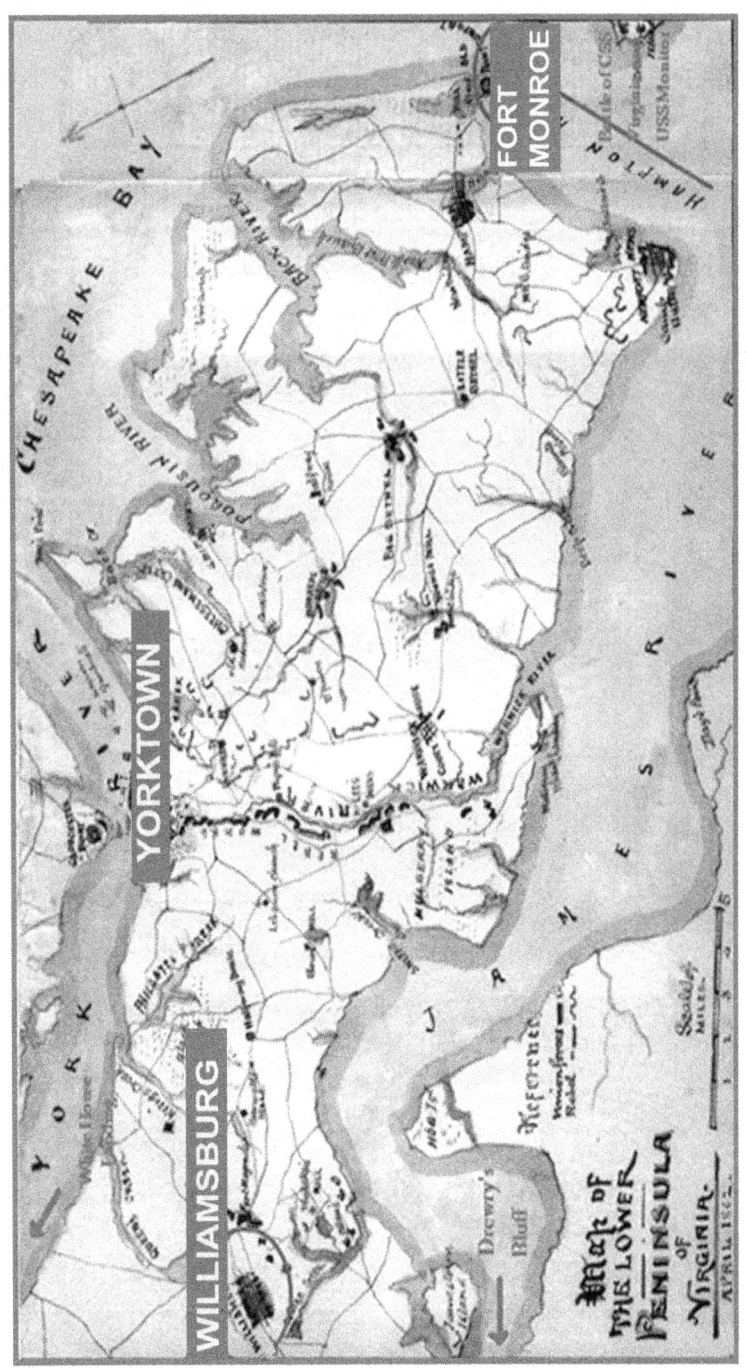

The Army of the Potomac's advance from Fort Monroe up the Virginia Peninsula was slow going. McClellan's plan for a rapid seizure of Yorktown was foiled when he discovered that the Confederates had established a fortified troop line stretched across the Peninsula (the Warwick Line). What he did not comprehend was how thinly stretched that line of troops was.

In fact, Yorktown commander, Confederate General John B. "Prince John" Magruder, defended the Peninsula against McClellan's available forces of 120,000 with a relatively meager force of only 11,000 to 13,000. An amateur actor before the war, Magruder created the impression of many troops behind the lines and of reinforcements arriving by marching small groups of the same men repeatedly in view from a distance or just out of sight, accompanied by plenty of noise and showmanship.

Confederate General
"Prince John" Magruder

Once again, McClellan was deceived into believing he faced a superior force and decided on a siege of the city. This required considerable preparation, and set the push towards Richmond back by several weeks.

McClellan's troops began to dig in, while a massive military force, including heavy artillery and mortars, was assembled to pound Yorktown into submission. But the delay in the Union attack enabled Confederate General Johnston to complete the return of his troops from Manassas, Centreville and Fredericksburg and to bolster

Magruder's forces. By mid-April, Confederate forces had swollen to 35,000 men and by the end of April there were 57,000, now under Johnston's direct command. McClellan's procrastination had enabled an extra 45,000 Confederates to be arrayed against him. But even then this was far fewer than the 100,000 which McClellan claimed opposed him, and still well short of the troops which McClellan had available.

After a month of preparation, the artillery assault was planned to commence on May 5. But Confederate General Johnston realized they would struggle against the massed artillery and on the night of May 3 stealthily withdrew his forces up the Peninsula towards Williamsburg.

The month-long siege resulted in 182 Union casualties and 300 Confederate casualties. But, very importantly for what was to come, it gave the Confederates time to regroup and build their defenses around Richmond.

With the Confederates gone, the only option for the Union was to give chase – the mass of heavy artillery so painstakingly positioned in front of Yorktown was useless. After skirmishing between their opposing cavalry forces, Johnston left behind a rearguard in fortifications near Williamsburg to allow time for the rest of his forces to escape. On May 5, the two armies clashed at the *Battle of Williamsburg* (also known as the *Battle of Fort Magruder*).

Ultimately 40,000 Union troops and 30,000 Confederates were engaged in the battle, with casualties and losses put at 2,283 for the Union and 1,682 for the Confederates.

The results of the battle were considered inconclusive: McClellan proclaimed it a "brilliant victory", but the Confederates considered that it successfully delayed the Union army and enabled the bulk of its troops to move past Williamsburg to Richmond's outer defenses.

Another skirmish occurred at Eltham's Landing, opposite West Point on the York River, on May 7, where troops sent by McClellan by boat came ashore and clashed with Confederate Forces. However, once again this engagement did not succeed in slowing the Confederate withdrawal towards Richmond.

McClellan had also placed hopes on a simultaneous naval attack on Richmond via the James River to the south. That approach was tested at the *Battle of Drewry's Bluff*, about seven miles downstream from the Confederate capital. On May 11, the Confederates scuttled their ironclad, *CSS Virginia*, concerned it would become stranded in the shallows of the James River and fall into Federal hands. Four days later, on May 15, five Union Navy warships, including USS ironclads *Monitor* and *Galena*, then led an assault on Fort Darling at Drewry's Bluff.

The Confederate artillery was positioned high above a bend in the river, and was able to shoot down on the approaching vessels, whereas the warships had difficulty in elevating their guns to shoot back and were hampered by sunken ships and other debris positioned in the river to block their passage. The Confederate guns severely damaged the *Galena*, inflicting heavy casualties, and the James River approach to Richmond was effectively closed.

Turret and deck of the *USS Monitor* – the U.S. Navy's first ironclad warship The visible damage to the turret came from the *Battle of Hampton Roads* between the *Monitor* and the *CSS Virginia* on March 9 – the first battle in history fought between iron clad warships. See pages 46-47.

THE VALLEY CAMPAIGN: PART 2

Back in the Shenandoah Valley, Jackson's Army of the Valley had been enlarged to two Divisions – "Jackson's Division" and the 2nd Division, commanded by Major General Richard S. Ewell.

The Union forces were divided in several locations in the Valley and, in early May, Jackson began an offensive to separately attack their different positions with as much of his combined force as he could – to fight them in pieces rather than collectively. By pushing his troops rapidly through the days and nights, he was able to launch attacks which drove the Federals back down the Valley. His tactics were so successful that in late May, Jackson's forces drove Banks from Winchester, out of the Shenandoah Valley and back across the Potomac into Maryland.

With McClellan's removal as General-in-Chief, Lincoln still was exercising day-to-day responsibility for the Army. Seeing Banks in retreat, and worried about the safety of Washington, Lincoln determined that he had to go on the offensive against Jackson. On May 24, he ordered reinforcements to join Banks, including Frémont from Western Virginia. Lincoln also sent orders to McDowell at Fredericksburg:

"You are instructed, laying aside for the present the movement on Richmond, to put 20,000 men in motion at once for the Shenandoah, moving on the line or in advance of the line of the Manassas Gap Railroad. Your object will be to capture the forces of Jackson and Ewell, either in cooperation with General Frémont or in case want of supplies or of transportation interferes with his movement, it is believed that the force with which you move will be sufficient to accomplish the object alone."[39]

On the same day, Lincoln also telegraphed to McClellan:

"In consequence of General Banks's critical position I have been compelled to suspend General McDowell's movements to you. The enemy are making a desperate push upon Harper's Ferry, and we are trying to throw Frémont's force and part of McDowell's in their rear."[40]

---

[39] OR, Vol 12, Part 3 - Correspondence, p 219
[40] OR, Vol 11, Part 1, p 30

Reluctantly McDowell sent the division of Brigadier General James Shields, which had only joined him from Banks's army in April, marching back to the Valley. In correspondence with Lincoln, McDowell described the move as *"a crushing blow to us"*, to which Lincoln responded, *"The change was as painful to me as it can possibly be to you or to any one."*[41]

McDowell then sent a second division, commanded by Major General Edward O. C. Ord, as further reinforcements for the Valley. Ord had been commander of McCall's 3rd Brigade of the Pennsylvania Reserves and had just been promoted to Division commander following his outstanding performance at Dranesville.

Banks's reinforced troops pursued Jackson south up the Shenandoah Valley until June 9 when at the *Battle of Port Republic* the Federals again were driven back and forced to withdraw.

The Union forces had been divided: the three Armies of Banks, Frémont and McDowell had operated separately in attempting to defeat Jackson's combined force, and Jackson had used that lack of cohesion to his advantage by attacking them separately. Lincoln learnt from this defeat by a smaller, faster moving and combined force and soon afterwards combined the three separate forces along with other troops around Washington into the Army of Virginia.

Jackson had spent six weeks harassing and skirmishing with the Federals, marching his 17,000 men 646 miles in 48 days and winning several minor battles as they successfully engaged 52,000 men from three Union Armies, and prevented them from reinforcing the Union offensive against Richmond.

Jackson had succeeded. McDowell's I Corps had been severely depleted, not by casualties but by having to provide reinforcements that made any advance from the north on Richmond to support McClellan that much harder.

His mission accomplished, at Lee's command, on June 18, Jackson turned his exhausted troops towards the Virginia Peninsula, the defense of Richmond, and the *Seven Days Battles*.

---

[41] OR, Vol. 12, Part 3 – Correspondence, p 220

General Richard S. Ewell who commanded the second Division of Jackson's forces in the Valley Campaign and ultimately became the third highest ranking officer in the Confederate Army

- *the 26* General Ranels crossed the rappihanock and we passed thru Fredericksburg. it is a nice town with beautiful shade trees along the Streets	On May 26, Reynolds's Brigade crossed the river, marched through Fredericksburg, and encamped about a mile and a half beyond. General Reynolds was appointed Military Governor, and his brigade performed duty as provost guard until May 31.

- the 27

I was down to see the Monument of Mrs Washington the mother of Gen George Washington. it has been spoilt by shooting at it and braking the corners. it is not finished yet. the monument is to the Write of Fredericksburg where the Gorden Family is Buryed. There is a Brick wall Built around the gravs of the Gorden Family with an iron gate on it

- the 28

to day we was on drill. it rained sum. it is a nice eavening. we are grazing our horsis while i write these few lines

- the 29

it is worm to day and we sined the Payroals and we got Payd of in the eavening

- the 30

it is worm this morning and i am on guard. in the eavening it rained

- the 31

in the morning it rained and we got orders to harnis up our horsis and move across the river

---

Mary Ball Washington lived in Fredericksburg from 1772 until her death in 1789 – soon after her son was inaugurated as the first President of the United States. A monument to Mrs. Washington was erected in Fredericksburg in 1833 and dedicated by President Andrew Jackson.

The monument was left unfinished until a women's organization formed in the late nineteenth century and raised money for a new memorial. That memorial was dedicated by President Grover Cleveland in 1894.

Reynolds's Brigade re-crossed the river, and again encamped near Falmouth.

THE PENINSULA CAMPAIGN: PART 2
Battle of Hanover Court House
May 27, 1862

On the Peninsula, McClellan's Army had undergone a reorganization, with the original three Corps available to him (II, III, and IV) expanded to five Corps. Brigadier General William Franklin, fresh from McDowell's Corps, was named commander of a new VI Corps with two Divisions – his 1st Division, now commanded by Brigadier General Henry Slocum, and Brigadier General William "Baldy" Smith's 2nd Division (from Keyes's IV Corps, which was reduced to two Divisions).

VI Corps' Franklin

1st Division's Slocum

2nd Division's Smith

Brigadier General Fitz John Porter was promoted to commander of a new V Corps. Porter's 1st Division, previously part of III Corps, transferred with Porter and was given a new commander in Brigadier General George W. Morrell. It became the 1st Division in Porter's V Corps. Major General George Sykes's division of U.S. Regular troops, formerly in the Reserve, became the 2nd Division. When McCall's Pennsylvania Reserves arrived, they would become the 3rd Division in Porter's V Corps.

V Corps' Porter

1st Division's Morrell   2nd Division's Sykes   3rd Division's McCall

Porter's newly formed V Corps (minus McCall's Pennsylvanians) was first tested at the *Battle of Hanover Courthouse* on May 27. Porter was positioned north of the Rappahannock River around Mechanicsville, with Confederate General Johnston's forces supposedly all south of the river around Richmond, when McClellan learnt of the presence of Confederate troops north of Mechanicsville at Hanover Courthouse.

Keen to keep his right flank free from any flanking movement, as well as to keep the way open for McDowell's forces to arrive from the north, McClellan sent Porter to investigate.

In a disorganized fight at Peake's Crossing, where the Confederates had been sent to guard the Virginia Central Railroad, Porter's 12,000 troops ultimately drove off the 4,000 Confederate troops but not without serious damage to the 44th New York Regiment from Morrell's 1st Division which suffered 25% casualties and had 44 bullet holes shot through its flag.

Estimates of Union casualties vary, from 355 (62 killed, 233 wounded, 70 captured) to 397. The Confederates lost about 200 killed and 730 captured by Porter's cavalry.

One of the important impacts of the battle was that, with Porter away to the north, McClellan was reluctant to move further troops south of the Chickahominy River, to strengthen the Union forces arrayed in front of Richmond. Thus this left open another tactical opportunity for the Confederates.

Commencement of the *Battle of Hanover Court House*, 1:45 pm.
Alfred R. Waud, artist, May 27, 1862.

Battle of Seven Pines (Fair Oaks)
May 31-June 1, 1862

With the Confederate withdrawal from Yorktown to the outskirts of Richmond, McClellan's troops had slowly worked their way up the Peninsula. The York River was under Federal control, enabling troops to be moved by boat up the river, past Eltham's Landing and West Point to McClellan's new base at White House Landing, upstream on the Pamunkey River, a tributary of the York. White House Landing (a plantation owned by W.H.F. "Rooney" Lee, son of General Robert E. Lee, and now a Confederate Army officer) was ideally located on the Richmond and York River Railroad which would enable McClellan to move his heavy siege equipment to the doors of Richmond.

By May 31, McClellan's forces were within four miles of Richmond, split to the north and the south of the Chickahominy River, which flowed into the James River further south. It was not ideal – it was wet season, the river was flooded, and the Confederates saw the Chickahominy and its swampy surroundings as a natural barrier against attack.

But McClellan decided on splitting his troops on either side of the river, first because he believed it gave him a strategic advantage to flank Confederate General Johnston's troops, and second because he was still expecting McDowell to arrive from the north with reinforcements and he wanted to keep the northern route open.

McClellan positioned his II, V, and VI Corps north of the river, and his III and IV Corps south of the river, with Keyes's IV Corps particularly far forward and close to Confederate lines.

Johnston realized that, with just 60,000 troops, Richmond could not withstand a prolonged siege against a far larger force, and decided to go on the offensive. At first he considered attacking the forces north of the Chickahominy, to weaken their position before McDowell arrived from Fredericksburg. Then on May 27, as Porter's V Corps was off to the north at the *Battle of Hanover Courthouse*, Johnston learnt that McDowell had been forced to send the bulk of his troops to the Shenandoah Valley, was returning to Fredericksburg and would not be arriving to reinforce McClellan at any time soon. He therefore decided to attack the more vulnerable and smaller force south of the river, with the intent of defeating them before the troops to the north could find a way to cross the flooding river and support them.

Johnston's attack on May 31 eventually pushed the Union troops back from their positions. But they were then able to hold their line, thanks to a large degree to reinforcements from Sumner's II Corps who managed to cross the river on the Grapevine Bridge which was near collapse in the flooded river – indeed, once they were across the river, the bridge was swept away. The fighting resumed the next day but the Union had brought up further reinforcements and the Confederates were not able to push them back any further.

Union artillery battery with 3-inch ordnance guns at the *Battle of Fair Oaks*

The battle was seen as somewhat inconclusive. Both sides claimed victory and both sides suffered roughly similar numbers of casualties. Union casualties were 5,031 (790 killed, 3,594 wounded, 647 captured or missing) and Confederate casualties were 6,134 (980 killed, 4,749 wounded, 405 captured or missing). This was the second highest number of casualties in the war to date.

However the battle was significant for two important reasons. First, on the evening of the first day, General Johnston was seriously wounded and, at the end of the fighting on June 1, Confederate President Jefferson Davis named his military adviser, General Robert E. Lee, as commander of the Army of Northern Virginia. It would be a defining moment for the South.

Second, McClellan's advance on Richmond was halted and he was put on the defensive. He moved all of his troops except for Porter's V Corps south of the Chickahominy, and spent the next few weeks reorganizing for his planned siege and waiting for reinforcements, while Lee prepared to counter attack. It was the closest the Union would come to Richmond for another two long, bloody years.

General Robert E. Lee

- *June 8, 1862*
this day year ago we came in camp write on the Allegheny River near Pittsburgh Pa and to day our batery commands Fredericksburg Va under General Ranels an General McColl Devision Pennsylvania Reserve Core

This is a rare moment of expression from Private Dunnan, giving written recognition of just how far they had come and what they had achieved a year on into the war.

And finally: The Pennsylvania Reserves head to the Peninsula

Finally the day had arrived. On June 6, McDowell received orders from Secretary of War Stanton to send General McCall's Pennsylvania Reserves to the Peninsula to reinforce McClellan:

"*The President directs that McCall's division be sent by water to Major-General McClellan immediately, and that you place such force at Fredericksburg by the time McCall leaves there as may, in your judgment, be necessary to hold that place.*"[42]

On June 8, McDowell received further instructions that, even though his Corps had been reduced from four available Divisions to one, he should continue towards Richmond:

"*The Secretary of War directs that, having first provided adequately for the defense of the city of Washington and for holding the position at Fredericksburg, you operate with the residue of your force, as speedily as possible, in the direction of Richmond, to co-operate with Major-General McClellan, in accordance with the instructions heretofore given you.*"[43]

McDowell wrote to McClellan that day, advising that he still hoped to arrive in time to be of service:

"*McCall goes in advance by water. I will be with you in ten days with the remainder by land from Fredericksburg.*"[44]

It would never come to pass.

---

[42] OR, Vol. 11, Part 3, p 216
[43] OR, Vol. 11, Part 3, p 220
[44] OR, Vol. 11, Part 3, pp 221-222

- the 9

We left Falmouth and went to Grays Landing. it is a nice cuntry down the Rappihanock valley

- the 10

the Third Bregaid came down to day it rained all day

- the 13

we got a bord of the Hamor and laid out in the river all night

- the 14

this is a brite morning and we start down the Rappihanoc and they run a ground at four a clock

- the 15

they got of at five a clock and run to two a clock. the win across and the tug boat could not tow us into the Chesapeak Bay. We laid in the mouth of the Rappihanoc river at ancor

- the 16

they got started at one a clock and now we are going down the Chesapeak Bay

---

The Reserves marched about 10 miles along the banks of the Rappahannock to Gray's Landing where steamers and other vessels sent from Washington and Fort Monroe were assembled to transport McCall's Division of 10,000 men and his four batteries of light artillery to the Peninsula.

Among these was a vessel named the Hamor – probably named after Captain Ralph Hamor, a seafaring captain and one of the original colonists to settle in Virginia. On June 13, Battery B boarded the Hamor and travelled down the river and into Chesapeake Bay.

With the Union now in control of the York River, the steamers and barges were able to transport the Pennsylvanian Reserves up the river past Yorktown to the new base of the Army of the Potomac at White House Landing.

McCall's Pennsylvania Reserves joined Porter's V Corps as the 3rd Division, with Brigadier General Reynolds commanding the 1st Brigade, Brigadier

and at ten a clock we came to ancor in the york river. i was on guard to night

- the 17

they droad there ancor[45] in the morning and we started up the york river. we passed york town. it is a small town but it is wel fortified on both sides of the river. we came to the landing at night and we staid on the Boat to morning

- the 18

we come need to unlode in the morning and got thru in the eavening. we laid at the white house where Gen Washington was married and where he lived for five years

General Meade commanding the 2nd and Brigadier General Truman Seymour (the Division's former artillery commander who had replaced the promoted General Ord) commanding the 3rd Brigade.

Cooper's Battery was one of four batteries in McCall's artillery brigade, along with Hezekiah Easton's Battery A and Mark Kern's Battery G – both now long-time companions from the 1st Pennsylvania Artillery – and Battery C, 5th U.S. Light Artillery, under the command of Captain Henry V. De Hart.

Landing at White House, Pamunkey River

---

[45] They drew their anchor

Transports at White House Landing and the Army camp on shore

The prolonged delays were taking their toll. While McClellan obsessed on delusions about the size of the forces he faced, the weather turned hot and sultry, and soldiers who had been working hard to dig trenches and gun emplacements began to fall ill. There was little shelter, food and drinking water were poor, and the longer they remained in one location the worse it became because of poor sanitation. Dysentery, chronic diarrhea and even scurvy were rife, as was "Chickahominy Fever" – probably malaria, typhoid or typhus. By June 20, 11,000 men were unfit for duty due to illness.

- the 19

we left the White House and traveled about twenty five miles over sum rough rods

The Battery arrived at White House Landing on June 17, joining the Division at Mechanicsville on June 20. Here the battery was placed on picket in front of the town, and on the extreme right of

- the 20

we started this morning to join General Ranels Brigaid and we was sent out on Picket and we fired a few shots across the River

- the 21

we are laying at Mechanicks ville on the rode that leads to Fredericksburg. our batery throde sum shell across the river to day

- the 22

we were ordered up in the morning to harnis our Horses and hold our selves in rediness to march

- the 23

we were ordered up in the morning at 3 a clock and we laid to day light. No one section throde a few shell across the river and the hole Batry opened fire on the rebles brest work in

the Army. For several days defensive positions were constructed and the gunners practiced firing at the enemy's positions which were in clear view across the river. But they received no response.

In fact, Battery B had arrived just in time to meet Confederate General Robert E. Lee's counter attack, designed to drive the Union Army back down the Peninsula and destroy it before it could escape. This counter attack became known as the *Seven Days Battles*.

As Lee prepared, McClellan delayed and procrastinated, and the more McClellan procrastinated the better Lee was able to prepare.

On June 18, Lincoln telegrammed McClellan and inquired politely *"if I could know about what day you can attack Richmond"*, stating that he *"would be glad to be informed, if you think you can inform me with safety."*[46]

McClellan's response that day was that *"we shall fight the rebel army as soon as Providence will permit. We shall await only a favorable condition of the earth and sky and the completion of some necessary preliminaries."*[47]

Yet still McClellan continued to delay, sending Lincoln numerous

---

[46] OR, Vol. 11, Part 3, pp. 232-233
[47] Ibid p. 233

the after noon but did git now reply **- the 24** we were ordered up at one a clock in the morning and marched to miles and it was dark and raining sum. At day light we were ordered back to our old post	telegrams before, during and after the Seven Days calling for massive reinforcements of troops and guns, and stating that his army was up against *"vastly superior odds"*, there was a probability of *"being overwhelmed by 200,000"*, that he had at his disposal *"great inferiority in numbers"*, and that his troops were *"behaving superbly, but you must not expect them to contest too long against great odds."* So they sat, stalled, impotent, and ineffectual – all when McClellan had Lee's forces greatly outnumbered.

Soldiers from the 2nd Regiment in Reynolds's 1st Brigade

Map following page:
Journey of Battery B in the *Seven Days Battles* around Richmond, Va. - June 26 – July 1, 1862, and sites of various Peninsula battles. Adapted from *Johnson's Map of the Vicinity of Richmond and Peninsular Campaign in Virginia*, Library of Congress.

BATTERY B

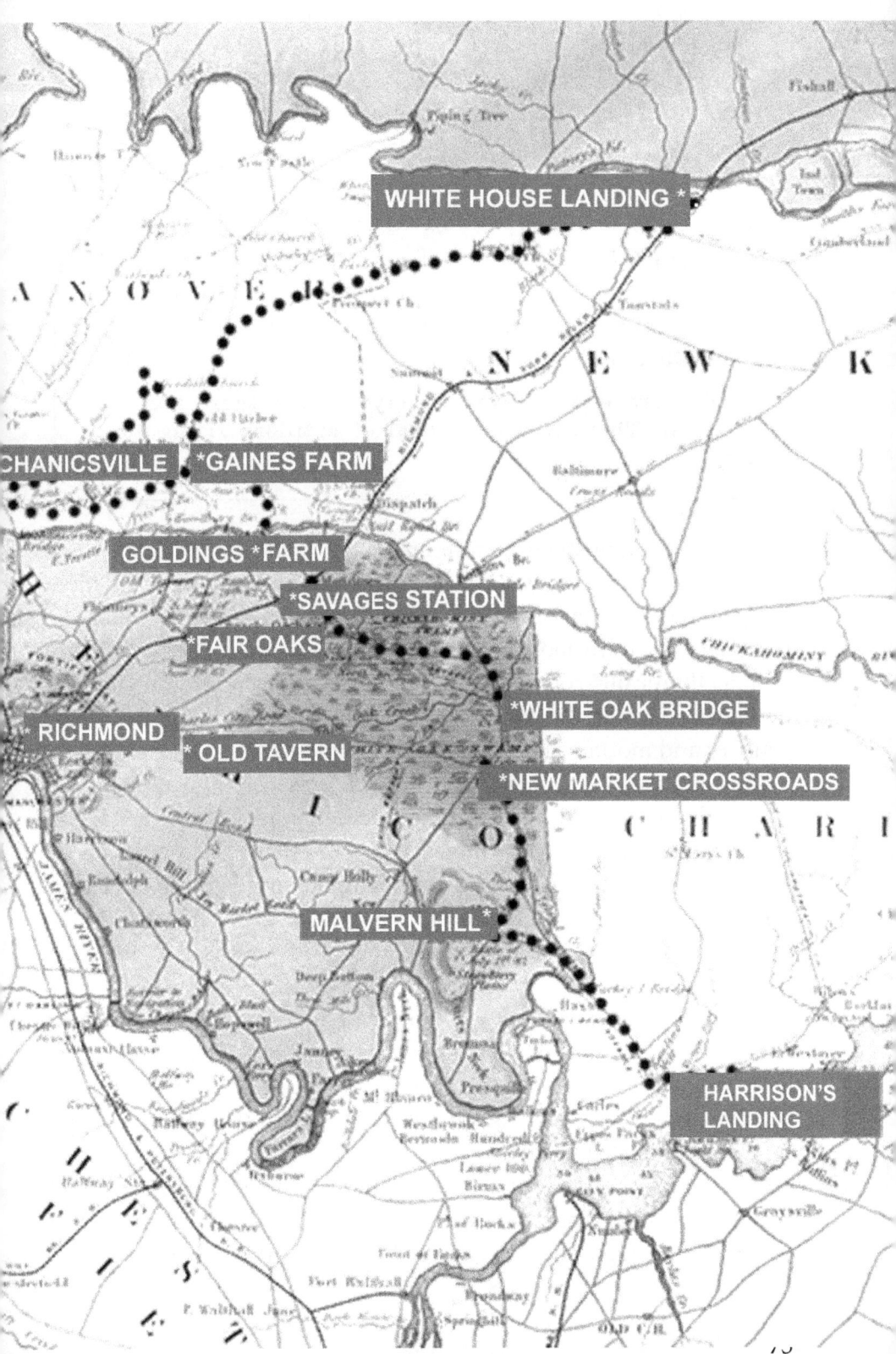

THE PENINSULA CAMPAIGN: PART 3

The Seven Days Battles: June 25 – July 1, 1862

DAY 1: WEDNESDAY, JUNE 25
Battle of Oak Grove

> - **the 25 June**
> the Drivers was relieved to day to give there horses sum rest. There is a good deal of artillery firing to day

A key distinguishing feature about the *Battle of Oak Grove* – the first of the *Seven Days Battles* – is that it was initiated by the Union. Despite the clear message from the *Battle of Seven Pines* that the Confederates were looking to take the offensive, McClellan slowly and methodically continued to prepare his positions for what he anticipated would be the siege of Richmond, bringing up heavy artillery and mortars and digging emplacements.

But after receiving news that Jackson was on his way from the Shenandoah Valley to reinforce Lee, McClellan realized he needed to take the offensive. He determined that he needed to close the arc of his front line around Richmond by moving his siege guns to a plateau near Old Tavern on the other side of a thick grove of trees – Oak Grove, which was cut in two by the headwaters of White Oak Swamp.

Heintzelman's III Corps was given the task and three Brigades – two from Brigadier General Joseph Hooker's 2nd Division and one from Brigadier General Philip Kearny's 3rd Division – were chosen for the attack against Confederate lines held by Major General Benjamin Huger's Division.

The attack commenced on the morning of June 25. While the left and center of the Union attack made some progress, their right flank struggled through the Confederate defenses, the swamp and the return fire. Huger then launched a Confederate counter-attack which drove back the Union's right flank. Heintzelman then went to send in reinforcements and at the same time consulted McClellan who was attempting to stay in touch with the battle by telegraph from three miles away. McClellan then told Heintzelman (to Heintzelman's surprise) to stop the counter-attack and withdraw his troops to their original trenches.

McClellan arrived at the front two and a half hours later, inspected the situation, realized it was not the impending disaster he feared it was developing into, and ordered the troops to move forward and retake the ground they had withdrawn from that morning. The fighting lasted until nightfall and still they did not reach the position McClellan had originally set out to take.

McClellan's assault gained him 600 yards at a cost of more than 600 casualties. The Confederate casualties were 440 (typically lower because they were defending rather than attacking).

It was the last offensive action McClellan would take against Richmond. From there on, he lost the initiative.

Confederate General
Benjamin Huger

DAY 2: THURSDAY JUNE 26
Battle of Beaver Dam Creek (Mechanicsville)

> **- the 26 June**
> To day at three a clock the rebles made there appearance on our rite at Mechanicksville and drove in our pickets. the Pennsylvania Reserve formed in line of battle and the Battle commenced. the Artillery opened there Deadly fire and drove them back. it lasted to ten in the eavening

The *Battle of Beaver Dam Creek* or *Mechanicsville* was the start of Confederate General Robert E. Lee's counter-attack – his plan to drive the Federals away from Richmond and to trap and destroy them on the Peninsula. McClellan's cautious, almost passive approach had given Lee ample time to prepare and plan for what would be his first battle as commander.

McClellan had moved two more of his Corps – Sumner's II Corps and Franklin's VI Corps – south of the Chickahominy River, to join Heintzelman's III and Keyes's IV Corps, with the intent of launching a further attack that day on Old Tavern, north of Oak Grove, to position his siege guns closer to Richmond.

That left Porter's V Corps isolated north of the river, around Mechanicsville. V Corps' troops were positioned in an L shape, with McCall's newly arrived 3rd Division facing west and being the most exposed to any attack from Richmond, while Sykes's and Morrell's Divisions were positioned along the north bank of the Chickahominy River, gazing across the river at the Confederate forces arrayed along the southern side.

Lee's plan was to use the 65,000 troops from the Divisions of his four principal generals – A. P. Hill, D. H. Hill, Stonewall Jackson and James Longstreet – to attack the 30,000 men of Porter's V Corps and drive them back along the north side of the Chickahominy River, cut off the Federal communications line to White House Landing and divide McClellan's army.

Confederate Generals A. P. Hill (left) and D. H. Hill were not related (although D. H. Hill was Stonewall Jackson's brother in law).

It was a risky plan: that left only two of Lee's Divisions – under Major Generals Benjamin Huger and John B. Magruder – south of the river and in front of Richmond: 25,000 men with the vast bulk of the Army of the Potomac in front of them. With more than 60,000 men south of the river, McClellan had them vastly outnumbered and a direct drive on Richmond was highly likely to be successful. But once again he did not take the initiative.

An important part of Lee's plan involved Jackson arriving with his troops from the Shenandoah Valley and attacking from behind Porter's right flank where Reynolds's 1st Brigade was positioned. Lee did not want a fight at Beaver Dam Creek – the Confederates had watched as the Pennsylvania Reserves had dug pits and built up barriers on the high slope in the days before the battle. Rather, Lee's plan was for Jackson's arrival to trigger a Union withdrawal from its well-defended position.

But Jackson ran late, Longstreet was delayed in crossing the Chickahominy, and neither participated in the battle. In the end it was the combined forces of A. P. Hill's Division and one brigade from the Division of D. H. Hill – about 10,000 men – which fought against McCall's Division and two brigades from Morrell's Division – about 15,000 men.

The battle began at 3 pm when, tired of waiting for Jackson's army to arrive, Confederate General A. P. Hill ordered his Division to cross the Chickahominy and advance towards Mechanicsville. In his report on the battle, A. P. Hill wrote, *"Three o'clock having arrived, and no intelligence from Jackson or Branch* (Brigadier General Lawrence Branch's Brigade, from Hill's Division, which was positioned closest to where Jackson was expected to appear, and was to link up with Jackson), *I determined to cross at once rather than hazard the failure of the whole plan by longer deferring it."*[48]

> Ambrose Powell Hill also carried a personal reason for taking the initiative against George McClellan's forces. In the late 1850s, A. P. Hill became engaged to Ellen Mary Marcy but her father opposed the idea and instead wanted her to wed McClellan, who had served under him in the regular army. Tearfully, Ellen Mary broke up with Hill and finally, after multiple marriage proposals, agreed to marry McClellan. During the Civil War, as A. P. Hill willingly lined up to be first to throw his troops into battle against McClellan's, the tale was later told of how the embattled soldiers would say, "Ellen, you should have married him!" Hill, who gained respect as one of the bravest and most aggressive Confederate Generals, was shot and killed on April 2, 1865, at Petersburg, seven days before Robert E. Lee surrendered.

Battery B moved with the general withdrawal from Mechanicsville to Beaver Dam Creek, which curves around Mechanicsville and which, with its high banks on the east side, created a natural moat from which to fire down on an enemy approaching across the fields and the swamps to the west.

On the right flank of the Union line, two sections (four guns) of Cooper's Battery took position on the right of Old Church Road behind the earthworks which had been dug in front of the rifle-pits of the Bucktails[49], with the majority of Reynolds's 1st Brigade. Those

---

[48] OR, Vol. 11, Part 2, p 835

[49] Soldiers recruited to the Bucktails – also called the 1st Rifles and 13th Pennsylvania Volunteer Infantry – earned eligibility for the regiment by demonstrating their expert marksmanship and, once accepted, then wore a buck's tail in their hats.

sections were led by Lieutenants Henry Danforth and Thomas Cadwalader (Private Robert Dunnan was in Cadwalader's section).

On Cooper's right, four guns from Kern's Battery G of the Pennsylvania Reserves were brought up soon after the battle commenced and on his left were two guns from Captain John R. Smead's Battery K, 5th US Regiment, from the Artillery Reserve.

In the center of the Union line were the two remaining guns from Kern's Battery G and De Hart's Battery C with parts of Reynolds's 1st Regiment and some of Seymour's 3rd Brigade. On the left flank with the remainder of Seymour's 3rd Brigade and Reynolds's 8th Regiment was Easton's Battery A from the Pennsylvania Reserves, and two more guns from Smead's Battery K. Finally, on the far left, on Old Cold Harbor Road, was Cooper's third section of two guns, commanded by Lieutenant James Fullerton, near Ellerson's Mill.

Most of Meade's Brigade was kept in reserve, although two regiments were thrown into the battle when fighting intensified on the left late in the day.

The artillery and troops were thus well positioned, dug in on high ground, behind the natural defenses afforded by the creek, associated swampy ground, and cut by ravines, with Lee's troops needing to advance over open ground. The approaching Confederate commanders knew they were at a distinct disadvantage.

As Union pickets withdrew from Mechanicsville as planned, they drew the Confederate army after them to the defenses at Beaver Dam Creek. On the left flank, Battery B's Lieutenant Fullerton opened the *Battle of Beaver Dam Creek* by firing the first artillery shots from the Union lines. Then all of the guns in line behind Beaver Dam Creek opened up a murderous fire on the approaching troops.

The main attack initially focused on the Union's right flank. Bates, in the *History of Pennsylvanian Volunteers*, states that *"the advance of the enemy was accompanied by a battery of horse artillery, which came forward on a gallop and attempted to come into position, but the fire from the guns of Battery B was so well directed that it left without unlimbering."*[50] This was probably Confederate Captain William J. Pegram's Virginia Battery which was forced back by heavy fire and then engaged in an ongoing

---

[50] *History of Pennsylvania Volunteers, 1861-65,* Samuel P. Bates, Harrisburg, Pa., p 1862

battle with three separate batteries. Pegram lost four of his six guns and 47 men that day.

On the Union's far right, Regiments from Confederate Brigadier General Joseph Anderson's Brigade of A. P. Hill's Division made an attack which initially drove back Reynolds's 1st Reserves. But Colonel William McCandless, from the 2nd Pennsylvania Reserves, then led a counter attack with reinforcements from two regiments of Brigadier General John Martindale's 1st Brigade in Morrell's Division. After hand-to-hand fighting, and aided by close-range double-canister from Kern's Battery, as well as from Cooper's Battery B, the Confederates were forced back from the Union breastworks.

Colonel William "Buck" McCandless (left), commander of the 2nd Pennsylvania Reserves, and Major Roy Stone, commander of the 13th Pennsylvania Reserves (Bucktails) both of which saw repeated action beside Cooper's Battery B during the war. Both regiments were a part of General Reynolds's Brigade.

This was the area where Lee had planned on a flanking movement from Jackson. It was the closest the Confederates would come to the Union line that day.

The Confederate Brigades led by Brigadier General James Archer and Brigadier General Charles Field from A. P. Hill's Division were being pounded by the artillery. So they decided that, even though they doubted their ability to cross the creek, their troops might be better protected up close to the Union line where the Union guns would be impeded by the presence of their own troops. They advanced against the right (the 13th and 5th Pennsylvania Reserves regiments from

Reynolds's Brigade) as well as a part of the center of the Union line, and into the face of the four guns positioned there from Cooper's Battery B, two from Kern's Battery G, and two from Smead's Battery K.

Several attempts to form a line of battle in front of McCall's line with the intention of capturing the batteries were unsuccessful, a concentrated fire of artillery, assisted by the infantry, cutting them down as fast as they could form. The slaughter here was described as *"terrible"*, with the gaps made in Confederate lines by the shots from the guns of Cooper, Kern and Smead distinctly visible.

Major Roy Stone, of the 13th Pennsylvania Reserve (the Bucktails), was stationed with Cooper and later wrote in his official report to Major General Porter about how under heavy waves of attack they had held what was apparently *"the key to the whole line."* Stone stated: *"For four hours the enemy made the most desperate effort to force their passage. Regiment after regiment was thrown forward for that purpose, but as often they melted away. The two sections of Captain Cooper's battery (B), Pennsylvania Reserve Corps, stationed in our earthworks, under Captain Cooper's command, were most bravely, skillfully, and effectively served, much of the time under your own direction. They drew the fire of the enemy's batteries, but the earth works and rifle pits gave great protection to the gunners and riflemen."*[51]

On the left of the Union line, at Ellerson's Mill, Brigadier General W. Dorsey Pender's Brigade from A. P. Hill's Division sent two Regiments to silence Lieutenant Fullerton's Battery B section and Smead's Battery K section. Despite the havoc caused by the four guns, one regiment made it to within 150 yards of the Union position but under the musketry of General Seymour's 12th Pennsylvania Reserves and General Meade's 7th Pennsylvania Reserves they withdrew with severe casualties.

By this time, Confederate General D. H. Hill's Division had begun to cross the Chickahominy River and Brigadier General Roswell Ripley's Brigade from D. H. Hill's Division was ordered to support Pender's Brigade and to try to turn the left flank of the Union forces. This was the worst Confederate mistake of the day.

Ripley's 44th Georgian Regiment led the charge directly towards Fullerton's Battery B section, with the 1st North Carolina Regiment behind them. The Georgians got as far as the creek – and then stood waist deep in the water firing up at the heavily defended Union positions. The North Carolinians got half way down the hill to the creek,

---

[51] OR, Volume XI Part II Page 414

could go no further with the 44th Georgian in front of them, and were stuck, caught in the open. The four guns from Batteries B and K poured canister into them as the 7th and 12th Pennsylvania Reserves fired on them. Finally, almost out of ammunition and soldiers, Ripley's forces withdrew. The 44th Georgia lost 335 men killed or wounded out of the 514 who participated in the charge. The 1st North Carolina lost 133 men killed or wounded out of about 500 men.

Ripley's 3rd North Carolina and 48th Georgia made a charge slightly further north, on the other side of Ellerson's Mill, but wisely stopped behind the mill race (the channel built to turn the mill water wheel) and suffered fewer casualties.

The firing along the line continued until after dark and finally ceased about 9 pm. McCall's Pennsylvanians bore the brunt of the attack and, using their high position across Beaver Dam Creek, had acquitted themselves well. Brigadier General Seymour subsequently generously offered much of the credit for the day's success to Reynolds whose *"study of the ground and ample preparation, even to the smallest detail, justify his high reputation as a soldier, and his conduct of the right wing is worthy of all praise."*[52] Ultimately, it was the superior performance of the Union artillery which had virtually guaranteed success.

Confederate General A. P. Hill later described how his troops acted gallantly *"in the face of murderous fire....the artillery fire from the enemy was terrific."*[53] Confederate Brigadier General Charles W. Field, commander of the 1st Brigade in Hill's Division, which led the assault on the center of the Federal line and took a dreadful pounding, commented that the artillery barrage across Beaver Dam Creek thinned his ranks with *"the most destructive cannonading I have yet known."*[54]

The battle resulted in a Union victory, with 360 Union casualties out of 15,000 troops engaged, and more than 1,400 Confederate casualties from the 10,000 troops engaged. McCall's Division lost about 300 men of the 8,000 who participated – 75 of them from the 13th Regiment (Bucktails) which had been positioned in front of Battery B.

For Battery B, Private Edward Smoot was killed, while Private Thomas W. Tait died of his wounds on July 4. Among those wounded were Sergeant James T. Nesbit, descendent of pioneering settler John

---

[52] OR, Vol 11, Part 2, p 399
[53] OR, Vol 11, Part 2, p 835
[54] OR, Vol 11, Part 2, p 841

Nesbit who laid out the village of Mount Jackson in North Beaver Township in 1815 (James was wounded again at Fredericksburg on December 13, 1862), Private John Lamm who was discharged on December 30, 1862, for wounds received at Beaver Dam Creek, Private John A. Meanor, and Private David B. Angus (who was also wounded at *Second Bull Run* on August 24, 1862). Tait, Nesbit, Lamm, Meanor and Angus were all members of the original Mt Jackson Guards. Another private, Peter G. Flaxenhart (the official rolls spell his name Flixenhart), was reported missing in action. He was potentially killed or captured: however there are no known records as to what happened to him.

Lee had lost his first battle as commander. Communication and coordination were poor, the battle plan complicated, and its execution unsuccessful. Only a part of his forces had even reached the battlefield. A. P. Hill's troops were shattered and vulnerable to a counter attack, while south of the Chickahominy the outnumbered forces Lee had left behind in front of Richmond presented only a thin line of defense.

Yet McClellan had not attacked Old Tavern as planned that day – he waited and waited, even though the *Battle of Beaver Dam Creek* did not commence until 3 pm, and he had plenty of time to take the initiative. And even with victory on the day he did not capitalize on that success. Despite the urging of some of his generals, McClellan would not launch a direct attack against Richmond: instead he withdrew to the southeast. Much to the confusion of many of those around him, the hope of taking Richmond and ending the war was fast disappearing.

J. Anderson

J. Archer

C.W. Field

W.D. Pender

R. Ripley

DAVID BUTT

To: Capt. JAMES C. CLARK, Assistant Adjutant-General

Official Report of Capt. James H. Cooper, Battery B, First Light Artillery, of the *Battle of Mechanicsville*:

Being on picket duty near Mechanicsville, I was ordered at noon on Thursday, June 26, to place my battery in position by General Seymour. The right and center sections, commanded by Lieutenants Danforth and Cadwalader respectively, were placed behind a half-finished earthwork on the right of the village, and the left section, commanded by Lieutenant Fullerton, in rear of the village near the church. By a subsequent order from General Reynolds, the right and center sections were placed behind an earthwork in camp of the Bucktails, and the left section in the rear of the Twelfth Regiment Pennsylvania Reserve Volunteer Corps rifle pits.

At 3 p.m. the enemy, consisting of a regiment of infantry, attempted to cross the field in our front, when we opened fire on them, and caused them to retire in confusion and disorder, when a battery of rifled guns opened upon us from a concealed position on the right. We returned the fire with marked effect, forcing them to change their position to the left of the field in our front. At this juncture of affairs they opened fire with a battery of smooth-bore guns from the woods directly in our front, which did but little injury, their shots all falling short.

At intervals during the engagement we fired canister into the woods on our right and left, assisting the First Regiment on our right and the Fifth on our left in repelling the enemy, who were engaging these regiments at short musketry-range.

The rifled battery continued to engage us until 8 o'clock p.m., when we ceased firing, having fired 800 or 900 rounds of shot, shell, and canister.

Lieutenant Fullerton, in command of the left section, reports having engaged the enemy at the same time, repulsing them with case-shot and canister. Four desperate efforts were made to cross the bridge near the mill, but as often were they repulsed and forced to fall back.

Respectfully, your humble servant,
J. H. COOPER,
Captain, Pennsylvania Artillery, Comdg. Battery B.[55]

---

[55] OR, Volume XI, Part 2, pp. 409-410

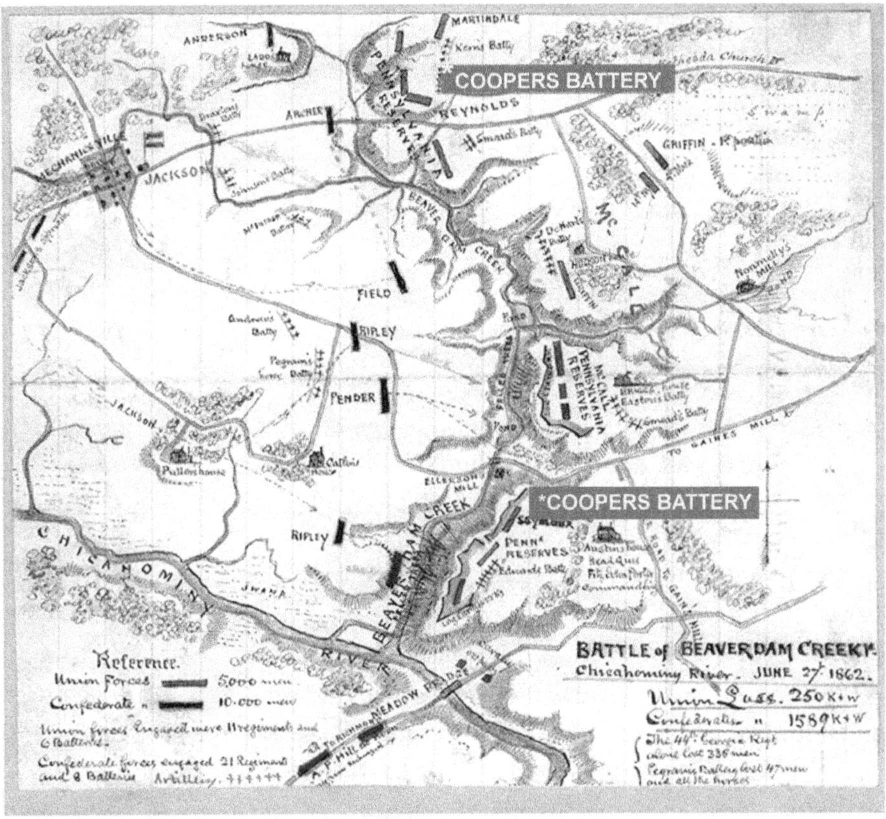

Cooper's Battery in two locations at the *Battle of Beaver Dam Creek*: two sections (four guns) just north of Old Church Road and one section (two guns) just south of Old Cold Harbor Road (the road to Gaines's Mill). The date on the map should read June 26, 1862.

Ellerson's Mill at Beaver Dam Creek

DAY 3: FRIDAY JUNE 27
Battle of Gaines's Mill

> *- the 27 June*
> *the battle was renued in the morning with great vigor. we got orders to fall back about four miles to Gaines Hill. here the battle was renued at three a clock and it lasted to dark wit great slauter on boath sides. Coopers Batry had to cover the retreat on theas two fites. we laid on a hill about half a mile from the Battle field and we cross the river about one a clock*

Despite the overwhelming Union success at Beaver Dam Creek, McClellan decided to pull back, and in effect committed to take his troops south to establish a new base on the James River. This meant abandoning White House Landing on the Pamunkey – and in turn abandoning any hope of taking Richmond, as the river and rail from White House Landing were vital to bringing McClellan's heavy artillery to the front. (Despite the length of time the Federals had spent on Richmond's doorsteps, McClellan had still not brought up all the siege weapons he considered he needed).

Still north of the Chickahominy River, Porter's V Corps was ordered to serve as the rear guard for the Army, to give the other Corps time to take their troops and wagons south. It was a decision which, for the second day running, would put V Corps and Battery B on the front line against the attacking Confederates in what would turn out to be the largest Confederate attack of the war and the bloodiest battle of the Seven Days.

Before dawn, as V Corps fell back from Beaver Dam Creek to establish a new defensive line still north of the Chickahominy, the right and center sections of Cooper's Battery remained behind with three regiments of McCall's infantry – the 9th, 12th, and 13th – to protect the rear (Fullerton's left gun section withdrew with the remainder of the army). Private Dunnan was with Cooper's remaining four guns which commenced firing at daylight and continued the barrage for over an hour. Confederate General A. P.

Hill is said to have been woken by an artillery round which passed straight through his room. The Confederates fired back with artillery which had been moved closer to the front line, and Cooper's gunners had to crouch on their knees to load.

The guns were limbered up and withdrawn a few minutes before the Confederate cavalry, attacking from the right, captured a part of the Bucktails regiment in the rifle-pits in front of where the guns had been.[56] Cooper's Battery then rejoined the Pennsylvanian Reserves on Gaines's Farm.

Once again Porter had established a strong position – this time on a plateau overlooking Boatswain's Creek and the surrounding swamp. Porter formed his two Divisions which had seen little fighting the previous day – Morrell's 1st Division and Sykes's 2nd Division – in the front line in a semi-circle facing the Confederate advance, with Morrell on the left and Sykes on the right, and the artillery on the plateau behind and above them, thus enabling it to fire over their own troops. McCall's already bloodied Pennsylvanians were positioned in reserve behind that line. Reynolds was on the right and Meade on the left, with Seymour's Brigade in reserve just behind them, and their batteries arrayed in front of them. Cooper's battery was on the right, overlooking open ground toward Cold Harbor, and the batteries of De Hart, Easton, and Kern on the left, their guns sweeping from commanding ridges over the space between the woods and the Chickahominy.

Behind them was open ground and roads leading to the bridges over the Chickahominy – vital access as either an escape route for V Corps or the gateway for reinforcements from south of the river.

---

[56] Parts of Companies K, D and E of the Bucktails tried to hide in Beaver Dam Creek swamp when they realized they were cut off. But as the Confederates closed in they hid their Brigade colors – their flag – in a hollow log. The Confederates discovered the flag and upon the fall of Richmond in 1865 it was found in the attic of the Confederate Capitol building. The flag passed into the hands of General Edward Ord and on his death in 1899 was placed on permanent loan to the Smithsonian Institute in Washington where it remained for more than a century. It was finally returned to Pennsylvania in 2003, and is on display in the flag conservation and storage facility near the Pennsylvania Capitol Building in Harrisburg.

Early in the morning, Porter sent McClellan a request for reinforcements. But after initially agreeing to send Brigadier General Henry W. Slocum's 1st Division from Franklin's VI Corps to reinforce the line, McClellan changed his mind and held off, fearing once again that his forces south of the river faced overwhelming odds. It was only after the battle had commenced and he received another request from Porter for reinforcements that McClellan sent Slocum's 8,400 men. Late in the day, following a third request from Porter, he also sent the brigades of Brigadier Generals Thomas F. Meagher and William H. French from Sumner's II Corps, but they arrived too late to help other than as a rear guard for Porter's retreat.

Thus this was a rare occasion where the Union forces of 34,000 were outnumbered by the attacking Confederate forces of 57,000, because most of the Union troops were camped in relative safety south of the river.[57] Yet Porter's strong defensive position, superiority (again) of his artillery, and disjointed attack from the Confederates (including another late arrival by Jackson's forces) meant the Union troops held their position and inflicted heavy casualties on the Confederates despite repeated attacks throughout the afternoon.

The first wave of attacks occurred early in the afternoon and McCall's Division was quickly brought into action, the batteries firing over the heads of the Federal forces in front of them, and the infantry thrown in to plug gaps and weaknesses in the front line. General Truman Seymour, in his report as acting Division commander at Harrison's Landing on July 15, described the action as follows:

> "The engagement commenced fiercely about 3 o'clock, and such overpowering numbers were brought into action by the enemy that it was soon necessary to send forward this division in support of the line already engaged. Regiment after regiment advanced, relieved regiments in front, in turn withstood, checked, repelled, or drove the enemy, and retired, their ammunition being exhausted, to breathe a few moments, to fill their cartridge boxes, again to return to the contested woods. Some of these regiments stood for four hours, scarcely changing position, yielding to no odds, and to drive the enemy in his turn. The woods were strewn with the

---

[57] The Confederates also now had access to a hot air balloon – the *Gazelle* – to observe Union troop movements, the *Battle of Gaines's Mill* thus making history as the first time two warring enemies used "air support" in battle.

heroic dead of both sides, and multitudes of wounded and dying painfully sought every hollow affording even momentary shelter from the incessant and pitiless fire." [58]

The initial Confederate assault was once again led by A. P. Hill's Division which attacked on the center and right of the Federal line against Brigadier General George Sykes's 2nd Division, made up of two brigades of US Army regulars – the 1st Brigade under Colonel Robert C. Buchanan and the 2nd Brigade under Lieutenant Colonel William Chapman – and the 3rd Brigade of New York volunteers under Colonel Gouverneur K. Warren.

Confederate Brigadier General Maxcy Gregg's South Carolina Brigade which had not taken part in the previous day's battle, led the assault and the 1st South Carolina reached the Federal line but then was driven back by withering fire and a strong counter attack involving savage hand to hand fighting. Further South Carolina regiments were thrown into the assault but the Union line held firm and Gregg's Brigade was shredded by cannon and rifle fire as it advanced and as it retreated – the Brigade lost 850 men killed and injured from 2,500 who engaged in the attack.

A. P. Hill then sent in Brigadier General Lawrence Branch's North Carolina Brigade, which also had missed the battle at Beaver Dam Creek, but they too were forced back. Finally the Brigades of Pender, Anderson, Archer and Field – all of which had suffered serious casualties at Beaver Dam Creek – were thrown into the fray on Gregg's right and the Union Army's center and left, defended by Morrell's 1st Division with the 1st Brigade commanded by Brigadier General John H. Martindale, the 2nd Brigade by Brigadier General Charles Griffin and the 3rd Brigade by Brigadier General Daniel Butterfield, made up of volunteer regiments from Maine, Michigan, New York, Massachusetts, and two regiments from Pennsylvania.

The Confederates charged across open ground – some regiments charged three times – against the lines held by Griffin's and Martindale's Brigades but the closest they came was to about 100 yards of the Union lines before they were driven back by heavy, well-directed cannon and musket fire.

---

[58] OR, Volume XI, Part II, Page 400

A. P. Hill had committed all six of his brigades and had gained nothing. Of 13,000 men in his Light Division, about 2,000 were killed or wounded – it was a resounding beating. In two days he had lost a quarter of his Division.

Confederate Generals Gregg and Branch

The second wave of attacks was led by Longstreet's Division, which was stationed to the far right of A. P. Hill – on the extreme left of the Union line which was held by Butterfield's 3rd Brigade. The fighting began about 5 p.m. as a diversionary tactic, with small attacks led by brigades commanded by Generals Cadmus M. Wilcox and George E. Pickett, but then developed into a full-scale assault, with General Richard R. Anderson's Brigade also thrown into the fray. Once again it was halted and held by the Union defense.

The first troops from Stonewall Jackson's Command, Ewell's Division, commanded by Major General Richard S. Ewell, had finally reached the battlefield (although Jackson and his Division were still coming up from the rear). Ewell's Division then attacked on A. P. Hill's right, but the strong Union defensive position once again pushed them back with heavy casualties. Among those casualties, almost half of the 250 troops from the 13th Virginia Regiment engaged in the battle were killed or wounded, with their Brigade commander, Brigadier General Arnold Elzey, shot in the head and seriously wounded. Elzey ultimately survived but never again took an active field command.

The three Brigades of the Pennsylvania Reserves were split up as the fighting wore on, with Regiments thrown into the front line as the need arose. The fighting was so fierce that muskets became overheated and began to foul up, and soldiers who ran out of ammunition either retired for more and rejoined the line or ended up using their muskets as clubs. The 5th and 13th Reserves from Reynolds's Brigade were said to have done so much firing that their hands blistered from the heat of the barrels. The casualty rate among officers also was high which weakened the leadership in the field.

Stonewall Jackson had finally arrived with the bulk of his Command, and Jackson's Division (headed by Brigadier General Charles S. Winder), along with D. H. Hill's Division and Brigadier General W. H. C. Whiting's Division from Jackson's Command, were also thrown into the battle. But still the Union army held.

Throughout the day the attacks had been piece-meal and unsynchronized: Confederate brigades were thrown at different parts of Porter's strongly held defenses at different times. The Confederates had failed to apply sustained pressure along the front and Porter was able to send reinforcements from McCall's Pennsylvanians and Slocum's 1st Division from VI Corps into the line as needed.

Finally at 7 pm Lee launched a coordinated assault along the entire two mile front of the Federal line. After what had been five hours of stubborn and very effective resistance, the Union troops were tiring, with increasing casualties, a shortage of ammunition and growing disorder in their lines. The break-through was finally made by Confederate Brigadier General John B. Hood's Texas Brigade from Brigadier General Whiting's Division in Jackson's Command. As the breakthrough gained momentum and the assault continued, the Union line began to fall back and then crumble.

The Federal positions began to topple like dominoes. As the Union troops retreated, they exposed McCall's four Batteries which were lined up side by side behind the front defensive line.

The first to be attacked was Easton's Battery A on the left, which repulsed the first assault, but was then overrun. Easton cheered and encouraged his men to fight on, shouting that they should never have his guns except over his body. Then Easton was killed and all his guns were captured.

Next in line was Kern's Battery G. Kern was wounded in the leg but continued to lead his men as they poured fire into repeated attacks. Finally the weight of numbers overran them, and Kern limbered up with four guns and retreated. Seven men were killed, twelve others were wounded, and two guns were left behind because the horses required to pull them had been shot.

De Hart's Battery C, 5th U.S. Light Artillery, was just to the right and was the next target of the attack. De Hart was wounded and carried away (he would later die of his injuries), and his place was taken by Lieutenant Ebon D. Scott. The battery was flanked and forced to flee, leaving behind three of their guns.

Finally there was Cooper's Battery B. The Battery poured a concentrated fire upon the advancing forces, causing them (as the pickets afterwards reported) to halt: the stubborn stand by Battery B was instrumental in giving the shattered remains of General Porter's Corps an opportunity to fall back. They continued to fire upon the attacking enemy, giving *"them the best we had"* with *"frightful effect"*. The battery held its position until a rebel charge was just a short distance away and a Union colonel called out, *"For God's sake, Captain Cooper, get your battery off or it will be taken in five minutes."* With Union forces withdrawing all around them, Battery B limbered up and escaped with all their guns.

The Union army retreated across the Chickahominy River, the retreat saved from being a rout by the arrival of Sumner's two Divisions and the dark of night which made pursuit hazardous.

In total, 19 of the 92 Union guns in action at Gaines's Mill were captured, half of them from McCall's batteries – a clear indication of their heavy engagement in the heat of the battle, and of how long and how bravely they held their line before trying to withdraw.

A report on the action that McCall's artillery faced is provided in *Echoes of Thunder: A Guide to the Seven Days Battles*: *"The fighting here was so fierce that of the four battery commanders only one would be standing at the end of the day (Cooper). One was killed outright, one died of wounds, and another was wounded."*[59]

Gaines's Mill was the worst battle of the Seven Days when measured by the number of casualties. From the 34,000 Union troops engaged, there were 6,837 casualties (894 killed, 3,107 wounded, and 2,836 captured or missing). Of the 57,000 Confederates engaged, their

---

[59] *"Echoes of Thunder: A Guide to the Seven Days Battles"*, Matt Spruill III, Matt Spruill IV, 2006, University of Tennessee Press, Knoxville, 2006, p196-198

casualties were 7,993 (1,483 killed, 6,402 wounded, 108 missing or captured). McCall's Pennsylvanian Reserves had lost another 1,651 men. About 25 percent of its capacity had gone in two days of battle. Slocum's Division, which entered the battle with about 8,400 men, had lost almost 2,000 men at Gaines's Mill alone.

During the night, Pennsylvania Reserves 1st Brigade commander, General John Reynolds, was captured when he fell asleep in a copse and woke in the morning to find he was behind enemy lines.

Despite the heavier casualties, this was a clear Confederate victory. Yet once again McClellan had missed a great opportunity: either to bring fresh troops north of the Chickahominy, reinforce the line and drive the Confederates back, or to attack Richmond's weakened defenses. McClellan simply refused to believe that so relatively few Confederate soldiers lay between him and Richmond – and was not prepared to test the strength of their defenses.

McClellan now had no option but to retreat further south, to the James River and safety. But with Lee's army in pursuit the Union Army's ability to escape was at severe risk.

Griffin, Martindale & Butterfield from Morrell's 1st Division, V Corps

To: Capt. JAMES C. CLARK, Assistant Adjutant- General

Official Report of Capt. James H. Cooper, Battery B, First Light Artillery, of the *Battle of Gaines's Mill*:

Having retired from Mechanicsville as rear guard of the division to Gaines Hill, at 3 p.m., we formed in line of battle with General Reynolds brigade in front of hospital buildings. Shortly afterward General Reynolds withdrew the infantry of his brigade, leaving for our support one regiment of New York troops. Remaining in this position until 5.30 p. m. the battery on our right retired, the enemy occupying their position, when we opened fire upon them and held them in check until 8 p.m. when, our support falling back, we retired in its rear to prevent the capture of our battery by a column of the enemy who were charging upon us. The effect of our shot on the enemy was destructive.

Respectfully, your humble servant,
J. H. COOPER
Captain, Pennsylvania Artillery, Comdg. Battery B.[60]

From Harper's Weekly – Battery fire at Gaines's Mill, 1861

---

[60] OR, Volume XI, Part 2, p 410

Confederate General Hood from Whiting's Division in Jackson's Command leads the charge at the breakthrough at Gaines's Mill

Grapevine Bridge across the Chickahominy – the retreat route for Battery B and McCall's Division

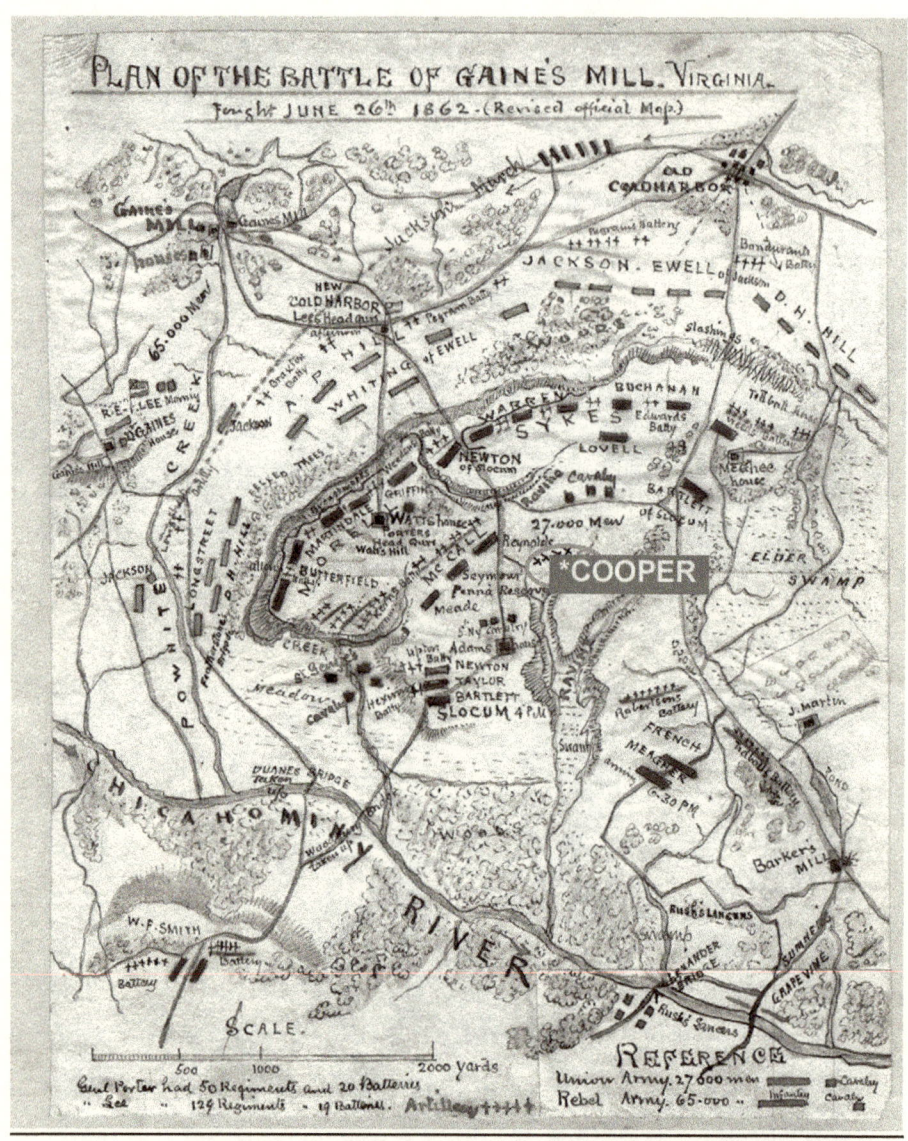

Cooper's Battery at the *Battle of Gaines's Mill* with the rest of McCall's Division and fellow Batteries to their left
The date on the map should read June 27, 1862.

DAY 4: SATURDAY JUNE 28
Battle of Garnett's and Golding's Farms

> *- the 28 June*
> we laid in camp all day to day and at dark we started for Saveg Station[61]. we traveled all night

While the *Battle at Gaines's Mill* was under way, a small battle occurred south of the Chickahominy when a Confederate brigade from Brigadier General John Magruder's Division turned a planned reconnaissance into a dusk attack on Brigadier General William F. "Baldy" Smith's 2nd Division from Franklin's VI Corps, and was quickly driven back. The scene was replayed the next day when again a supposed reconnaissance turned into an attack on the same forces at nearby Golding's Farm. Once again it was driven back and then a counter-attack followed.

The Union suffered 189 casualties and the Confederates 438.

While minor in substance, these raids did manage to heighten McClellan's anxiety and confirm his belief that he was going to be attacked from all directions, including by "superior forces" from south of the Chickahominy (particularly the assault on Garnett's Farm which occurred as the *Battle of Gaines's Mill* was still being slugged out). This strengthened both his reluctance to reinforce Porter and his desire to head towards the relative safety of the James River.

Battery B remained parked that day on Trent's Hill, on the south bank of the Chickahominy. That night the Pennsylvanian Reserves were ordered to move in the direction of White Oak Creek, but because of congestion on the roads due to the large numbers of retreating troops and, more importantly, columns of wagon trains, they spent all night marching, and did not reach White Oak Creek until near noon the next day.

---

[61] Savage's Station, scene of Day 5 of the *Seven Days Battles*.

DAY 5: SUNDAY JUNE 29
Battle of Savage's Station

> *- the 29 June*
> this morning found us on the road to about noon when we stopped to rest and at four a clock we were on the rode again. we drove to twelve a clock when we got orders that we was on the rong road. here we laid down on the road and went a sleep

While McClellan continued to withdraw towards the James River, by Day 5 much of his army was still caught in the vicinity of Savage's Station, a railroad crossing just south of the Chickahominy River which had been established as a major depot and field hospital. From there, the troops and their extraordinarily long wagon train of supplies had to find a way through or around White Oak Swamp to reach the roads which would take them south to the James.

Lee devised a pincer plan to try to trap the retreating army, but the plan was again poorly executed, in large part because Jackson was still north of the Chickahominy and failed to join up with the attacking forces.

Ultimately most of the battle occurred between Confederate Brigadier General John Magruder's Division and McClellan's rear guard – Sumner's II Corps.

The result was again inconclusive: the Union suffered about 1,000 casualties and also left behind 2,500 sick and wounded soldiers in the field hospital at Savage's Station. The Confederates had about 500 casualties, but Lee's trap had failed to close, and by midday the next day most of the Army of the Potomac had crossed White Oak Swamp.

This was the first battle in history in which cannon mounted on a moving train was used (by the Confederates).

At dark on June 29, Battery B's division moved out on the road beyond the junction of the New Market and Charles City Roads, and held the position there as defense for the hundreds of wagons using the roads behind them to head south. Private Dunnan's diary entry about how they *"laid down on the road and went a sleep"* demonstrates just how exhausted they already were: it was the first night's rest for them since the previous Wednesday. Yet the hardest day of all was still to arrive.

Savage's Station in a peaceful moment

Post-battle: Wounded men at the Savage's Station field hospital

DAY 6: MONDAY JUNE 30
Battle of Glendale

> **- the 30 June**
>
> they got the bois wake up and we counter marched and went back into a field. here we got our breakfast and fead our horses.
>
> We laid to thre a clock when we were formed in a line of battle. we were not long here when boom went a cannon and the ball passed over our batry.
>
> It was not long to our batry opened on them and silenced there guns. the Infantry came up and charged on us. we pored in the canister into them. they had to fall back. they came the second and third time with the same result.
>
> here the batry on our rite retreated and they directed there hole fire on us. here they made a rite flank movement and pored in a volley of musketry and shot down our horses and we were ordered to retreat leaving our Batry on the field here.
>
> we lost two of our Lieutenants, H T Danford and T Cadwalader.
>
> This was at the *Battle of White Oaks Swamps.*

The *Battle of Glendale,* is regarded as one of the great opportunities missed by the South throughout the entire war. The battle gave the Confederates their best chance yet to isolate and overrun much of the Army of the Potomac. But the attack failed.

The Union Army was continuing to withdraw towards the James River but the going was slow and there were huge bottle-necks in the poor roads around Glendale. Brigadier General Porter's V Corps (minus General McCall's 3rd Division of the Pennsylvania Reserves) had reached the relative safety of Malvern Hill near the river, but the remaining four Corps and McCall's Division – the bulk of McClellan's army – were still several miles away around Glendale and White Oak Swamp.

Lee's plan was to cut off the Union line of retreat by attacking simultaneously from three directions – with Jackson's troops from the North across White Oak Swamp, with Major General Benjamin Huger's Division along the Charles City Road in the north-west, and with Longstreet's and A. P. Hill's Divisions (now under the overall command of Longstreet) from the west along the Long Bridge Road (the Glendale end of New Market Road). Magruder's Command and Major General Theophilus Holmes's Division were to operate to the south, to attack the fleeing Federal wagon trains and to tie down and potentially attack the Union troops already gathering at Malvern Hill. The escape route would be cut, the Army of the Potomac would likely have been trapped and destroyed, and the way cleared for a Confederate advance on Washington.

After inspecting the troops that morning, McClellan departed to the safety of the *USS Galena* on the James River and did not set foot again that day on the battlefields around Glendale, nor on the next day at Malvern Hill. Curiously, nor did he name anyone to take overall command in the field, leaving four Corps commanders (and McCall) around Glendale to operate independently.

McCall had not expected his Division to be fighting that day. Already severely battered and depleted by days of intense fighting and marching, with little rest, shelter or food, he thought he was taking his Division south to join the rest of V Corps for a well-earned rest at Malvern Hill. McCall's three brigades had moved out from Glendale on the roads towards Richmond as a defense against any attack on the long line of wagons making their way towards the James. In the morning they were ordered back to the crossroads at Glendale. While resting and recuperating there, thinking they were next to head south, they realized there was a serious gap in the center of the Union's front line between Brigadier General Joseph Hooker's Second Division and Brigadier General Phillip Kearny's Third Division – both from Heintzelman's III Corps.

Joseph Hooker   Phillip Kearney

Truman Seymour later described what happened.

"Exhausted by the fatigues of the previous three days of fighting and nights of marching, men and officers courted this short rest with delight and reposed in fancied security. The order to follow the mass of the corps was momentarily expected by the men, and no dispositions were made to meet an attack, until General Meade and myself, riding to the front, found only a squadron of cavalry, unsupported by a single infantry soldier, interposing between the division and the enemy, whose pickets were close at hand. Reporting this to General McCall, the First Regiment, Colonel Roberts, and the Third, Colonel Sickel, were immediately ordered to the front on outpost duty, and the division was soon after posted in order of battle."[62]

So McCall's Division was then positioned on Long Bridge Road in front of Glendale – a vital junction expected to be the target of the Confederate attack from Longstreet and A. P. Hill which was aimed at breaking the Union line and dividing McClellan's army.

Taking this position was a risky decision. McCall had already lost 2,000 of his men in just two days of fighting, and the remaining 6,000 troops were exhausted and battle fatigued, with many of them now also falling physically ill. It was a huge gamble to expect them to hold the center of a combined attack by a larger force. And in reality there were fresher Divisions which had faced little or no fighting to date and which would have been far better placed to take McCall's

---

[62] OR, Volume XI, Part II, Page 401

position if the Federals had been properly organized and commanded.

Alanson Randol

McCall's two surviving batteries – Cooper's Battery B and Kern's Battery G (commanded by Lieutenant Frank P. Amsden with Kern absent wounded) – were joined by three batteries from the artillery reserve to form a new Artillery Brigade for the Pennsylvania Reserves: Lieutenant Alanson M. Randol's Battery E, 1st US Artillery, and Captain Otto Diederich's Battery A and Captain John Knieriem's Battery C of the 1st Battalion, New York Light Artillery. The five batteries were positioned across Long Bridge Road with the batteries running from left to right being Diederich, Knieriem, Cooper, Amsden and Randol.

They were supported by McCall's infantry, with Seymour's 3rd Brigade behind the batteries on the left and Meade's 2nd Brigade on the right. The 1st Brigade, now being commanded by Colonel Seneca Simmons of the 5th Pennsylvania Regiment following Reynolds's capture at Gaines's Mill, was in reserve.

Seneca Simmons

Of the position, McCall later wrote, *"The open front was about 800 yards; its depth about 1,000 yards. It was a beautiful battle ground, but too large for my force to find cover or protection on both flanks."*[63]

On McCall's left was Hooker's Division and on his right was Kearny's Division from Heintzelman's III Corps: the road and the fields created a perfect funnel to channel the attacking forces in towards the Pennsylvanians.

Slocum's 1st Division, from Franklin's VI Corps and which had taken a terrible battering at Gaines's Mill, was positioned to the right of Kearny, facing Confederate General Huger's Division to the northwest, while Brigadier General Baldy Smith's 2nd Division was positioned to the north (on Slocum's right) at White Oak Swamp Bridge, where Jackson was to attack. Brigadier General John Sedgwick's 2nd Division of Sumner's II Corps was placed in reserve behind McCall. However, when Jackson engaged at White Oak

---

[63] OR, Vol. 11, Part 2, p 389

Swamp Bridge, two of Sedgwick's three Brigades were sent north to support Smith.

Thus there was a rough semi-circle of Union Divisions arrayed around Glendale to face the enclosing Confederates: from left to right involving Hooker, McCall, Kearney, Slocum and Smith, with Sedgwick in reserve.

Once again, poor communication and coordination in Lee's ranks resulted in a poorly executed battle plan. Instead of a coordinated assault from all three directions at once against the Union forces, there was a disjointed, staggered attack. Jackson's command made a lackluster attempt to cross White Oak Swamp and Huger's Division, which was meant to open the battle, made a likewise feeble attempt to engage: both ended up in ineffective and irrelevant artillery duels. Further south, Confederate General Holmes's Division – the Department of North Carolina – engaged in a futile artillery exchange with Union guns on Malvern Hill which were aided by U.S. Navy gunboats on the James River. Magruder's Division spent most of the day marching: this was no fault of his own but rather a failure of command.

Hence while Lee planned to bring more than 60,000 troops to the battle, only Longstreet's and A. P. Hill's troops – about 19,500 in total – were properly engaged against about 23,500 Union troops (out of 55,000 in the area).

The fighting began with skirmishes and artillery exchanges as Longstreet waited for Jackson and Huger to push through from the north and northwest. But at about 4:00 pm, it was in fact Battery B which proved to be the catalyst in finally getting the real battle under way. When Longstreet ordered his artillery to fire on the Federal lines, Battery B returned the fire – and went close to blowing up Confederate President Jefferson Davis.

Davis and Lee were with Longstreet near the front line (they had moved back somewhat after being ordered to do so by A. P. Hill) when Battery B's shells burst nearby, wounding one man and three horses. A. P. Hill later noted: *"The fight commenced by fire from the enemy's artillery, which swept down the road, and from which His Excellency the President narrowly escaped accident."*[64]

---

[64] OR, Vol. 11, Part 2, p 838

Longstreet immediately ordered General Richard Anderson's Brigade of South Carolinians, now under the command of Colonel Micah Jenkins, (with Longstreet in overall command, Anderson was commanding Longstreet's Division) to silence Cooper's guns. While Longstreet had intended that this be achieved either through use of artillery or by sniper fire from Jenkins's Palmetto Sharpshooters, Jenkins instead led his full brigade in a frontal attack on Battery B. Thus the major battle was commenced – unplanned, uncoordinated, and disjointed.

Time after time the South Carolinians were driven back by barrages of grape and canister from Battery B, ably supported by Amsden's and Randol's guns, and the Pennsylvania Reserves infantry. Captain John Cuthbertson of the 9th Pennsylvania Reserves which was initially placed in support of Battery B, described the action as follows:

> "The enemy consumed a couple of hours in a number of ineffectual attempts to take this battery, several times charging up within a few yards of the guns, but each time driven back with great slaughter."[65]

Longstreet then sent in Generals James Kemper's and Cadmus Wilcox's Brigades to support Jenkins's attack. Ultimately 11 of the 12 Brigades from Longstreet's and Hill's Divisions were thrown into the battle, charging forward in three waves.

Micah Jenkins

Cadmus Wilcox

James Kemper

---

[65] OR, Vol. XI, Part 2, p 395

The fight continued throughout the late afternoon and into dusk, often breaking into hand-to-hand combat as opposing troops engaged at close quarters. Confederate General Edward Porter Alexander later noted:

"No more desperate encounter took place in the war and nowhere else, to my knowledge, so much actual personal fighting with bayonet and butt of gun."

Owing to the excessive heat of the guns due to rapid and prolonged firing at Beaver Dam Creek and Gaines's Mill, the vent-pieces of Battery B's guns had so melted that some of the vents were twice the original size. The guns were worked as rapidly as possible, but the size of the vents required the gunners to insert two primers in some of the guns, along with the one to which the lanyard hook was attached, to discharge the piece.

Then Amsden's Battery G ran out of ammunition – their caissons had been sent to the rear to protect them from the fighting and could not be found, and Amsden withdrew tearfully. That left a gap between Cooper and Randol on his right, on the other side of the Long Bridge Road. The Confederates attacked again and, despite the continued volleys of canister from Cooper's guns, the battery was overrun and Cooper's men were forced to retreat. With most of their horses dead, shot by the Palmetto Sharpshooters, the guns had to be abandoned.

Colonel C. Feger Jackson of the 9th Regiment, Pennsylvania Reserves (in Seymour's 3rd Brigade), was returning towards Battery B when he met up with Cooper who told Jackson that his battery had been captured.

"Finding that the men deeply sympathized with the captain in his loss, I at once determined to recapture the guns. A successful charge was made. The enemy was driven from the guns diagonally to the right and into the woods. I immediately commenced reforming my regiment on the road to our right. At this time a heavy firing was opened upon us from the right. We advanced into the woods, where skirmishing commenced and continued until after dark..... This was the most disastrous day of the

three, having a number of my most efficient line officers killed or wounded." [66]

The recapture of the battery had given Cooper enough time to carry off the dead and wounded. But it was a short reprieve. Confederate reinforcements from Wilcox's 4th Brigade of Alabamians then came up to take the place of the decimated South Carolinians and charged along the left and right sides of the road towards Randol's and Cooper's batteries.

After further fierce fighting, in which Randol's battery inflicted severe damage on Wilcox's 8th and 11th Alabamian Regiments, the battery was overrun by *"a perfect torrent of men"* and suffered severe casualties. General Meade, whose 2nd Brigade was supporting Randol, was seriously wounded in the arm, back and side during the attack but stayed on his horse and rode to the back of the lines for treatment.

McCall rode into the battle lines and endeavored to encourage the regiment to hold their ranks. Later he wrote:

"It was here my fortune to witness one of the fiercest bayonet fights that perhaps ever occurred on this continent. Bayonet wounds, mortal or slight, were given and received. I saw skulls crushed by the butts of muskets, and every effort made by either party in this life-or-death struggle, proving indeed that here Greek had met Greek." [67]

On the Confederates' right side of the road, Wilcox's 9th and 10th Alabamians drove Cooper and the supporting infantry back and retook the battery. But the Alabamians had sustained terrible casualties and further counter attacks forced them to withdraw.

But the tidal wave of Confederate reinforcements continued: in Wilcox's place came Charles Field's Brigade of Virginians from A. P. Hill's Division which again drove up each side of Long Bridge Road and claimed Randol's and Cooper's Batteries for a final time. The Confederates pushed on and drove the Union line back towards Willis Church Road – the main thoroughfare to Malvern Hill.

---

[66] OR, Volume XI, Part II, Page 422
[67] OR, Volume XI, Part II, Page 390

In the gathering gloom of nightfall, McCall was seeking to bring forward reinforcements when he rode into enemy lines (where not much earlier it had been his line) and was captured.

On the Union left, Kemper's Virginian Brigade from Longstreet's Division attacked McCall's 3rd Brigade led by Truman Seymour, which was positioned in support of Knieriem's and Diederich's Batteries. Reynolds's 1st Brigade of the Pennsylvania Reserves, now being led by Seneca Simmons, came up to reinforce Seymour, but the line broke, and infantry and gunners began to fall back. Two of Knieriem's guns were captured, but Diederich's battery was able to limber up and escape.

While the brunt of the attack was borne by McCall's division near the cross roads, Longstreet's and A. P. Hill's brigades were now attacking on a 2 mile front north and south of the Glendale intersection. On McCall's right flank, Kearny's 3rd Division held against repeated Confederate attacks with reinforcements from Union Brigadier General John C. Caldwell's 1st Brigade from Sumner's II Corps and two brigades from Slocum's 1st Division, IV Corps, which were able to be redirected into the line when Huger's attack did not materialize from the north-west. On the far left flank, Hooker's 2nd Division was also under pressure but repelled what were relatively smaller Confederate attacks.

But McCall's Pennsylvanians were breaking and falling back, being rallied and reorganized and then counter-attacking, before being pushed back again. They were exhausted, short of commanders and ammunition, and in danger of being completely overrun. There was little spark left in them. A gap was opening through the middle of the defensive line and the entire Union front was threatened.

As the left of McCall's line crumbled, the remaining Brigade which had been held in reserve – the 2nd Brigade under Brigadier General William W. Burns, from Sedgwick's 2nd Division of II Corps – was brought up to fill the gap. Then as Jackson had failed to mount a serious challenge at White Oak Swamp, Sedgwick's other two brigades were able to return to provide invaluable reinforcements and hold the line.

As nightfall came, the fighting died down, and the Union Army had held despite wave after wave of vicious, bloody attacks.

Major General Sedgwick would ultimately be the highest ranking Union casualty in the Civil War, killed by a sniper at the *Battle of Spotsylvania Court House* on May 9, 1864, seconds after uttering the famous quote, "They couldn't hit an elephant at this distance."

Stonewall Jackson did not cross White Oak Swamp that day and hence was unable to assist in fulfilling Lee's plans to attack and slow the retreating Union Army from the north. In fact, Jackson played a very minor role in the *Seven Days Battles*, with historians considering that his successful exploits in the Valley campaign and subsequent forced march to Richmond had left him exhausted, lethargic and potentially ill.

The relative inaction by Jackson and Huger freed up 10,000 Federal troops to go to the aid of the remaining Union forces. Without those reinforcements the outcome of the day could have been very different.

Among the Pennsylvanians, Division commander McCall was captured, 2nd Brigade commander Meade was seriously wounded, and Reynolds's replacement as 1st Brigade commander, Colonel Seneca G. Simmons, was mortally wounded when the Brigade was brought up to support Seymour's 3rd Brigade against Kemper's Virginian Brigade. Simmons was on his horse rallying his troops when he was shot, and he died later in hospital. After his death, Simmons's sword was presented to Confederate Colonel Micah Jenkins who had led the initial charge against Cooper's guns. Jenkins, by then a General, was still wearing the sword when he was killed at the *Battle of the Wilderness* on May 6, 1864.

In the same volley which mortally wounded Simmons, Seymour's horse was killed and fell on him, leaving Seymour dazed and confused and unable to continue his command. Later that night, having recovered sufficiently, Seymour was put in command of the Pennsylvania Reserves and led the withdrawal to Malvern Hill and subsequently to Harrison's Landing.

Battery B lost three killed and 10 wounded, among them their first Commander before Cooper, Lieutenant Henry T. Danforth, as well as Lieutenant Thomas Cadwalader – the Commanders of the center and right sections of the Battery B gun crews. Sergeant James S. Miller was also killed. Three of the 10 wounded subsequently died – Privates William N. Waldron who died on a date unknown, Franklin Johnston who died on July 24, and Isaac P. Wilson who lost a leg in the battle and died on August 24. All but Johnston and Waldron were original members of the Mt Jackson Guard.

Among the wounded were William W. Wallace, who was subsequently discharged on November 28, 1862, because of his wounds and Private David Brubach who lost his leg and was discharged on December 3, 1862. Also wounded were Sergeant John S. Hamill, Private (later Corporal) Joseph Buchanan, Private Cyrus W. Davis, Private Robert (Albert) Kennedy and Private William Fravel.

McCall's Division, already with almost 2,000 casualties, lost another 1,118 killed, wounded or missing.

The South Carolinian Brigade, which Confederate Colonel Micah Jenkins led in repeated charges against Battery B, lost 562 killed or wounded and 27 missing – almost half the brigade of about 1,200. Worst hit among these were the Palmetto Sharpshooters Regiment which lost 254 out of 375 men. Wilcox's Alabamian Brigade, which came up to reinforce Jenkins and at one stage took Cooper's guns, lost 471 men killed, wounded or missing out of about 1,850 men. Kemper's Virginian Brigade, which had attacked Seymour's line on the Union left, lost 414 of 1,443 men. In all, Longstreet lost more than a quarter of his division, most of them in the attack on McCall's Division and his batteries.

While reports on casualties at Glendale vary, a reasonable estimate is that the Union lost about 2,000 killed or wounded (297 killed and 1,696 wounded) while the Confederates lost almost 3,500 (638 killed and 2,814 wounded), with the difference largely due to the North's ability to bring its superior artillery into force at close range. The North lost a further 1,804 missing or captured, while the Confederates had 221 missing – largely evening out the losses for the North and South.

During the night, both sides did their best to deal with the damage done throughout the day in what is regarded as one of the most ferocious battles in the war. The cries of agony from the wounded still on the battlefield continued throughout the night and the surgeons honed their skills on countless amputations. In his official report, Union General Hooker, who had been on McCall's left, described the night as follows:

> *"From their torches we could see that the enemy was busy all night long in searching for his wounded, but up to daylight the following morning there had been no apparent diminution in the heart-rending cries and groans of his wounded. The unbroken, mournful wail of human suffering was all that we heard from Glendale during that long, dismal night."*[68]

Despite the carnage, the lines had moved very little, and many of the artillery pieces overrun during the day still sat on the battlefield. A number of the battery commands wanted to reclaim their guns but were told they could not, much to their severe disappointment.

While the battle was regarded as somewhat inconclusive, it was a victory to the Union in so far as it thwarted Lee's battle plans. McClellan's line had held, the roads to the south remained open, and the retreat was able to continue which enabled the entire Union Army to take up a strong defensive position at Malvern Hill.

McCall's Pennsylvanian Reserves had little fight left in them, but for most of the day had largely succeeded in holding the center of the Union line against successive attacks from a multitude of Confederate Brigades. As McCall pointed out:

> *"Lee's object in moving down the New Market Road was to break through the Union Army at that point, and taking possession of the Turkey Bridge road (or Willis Church Road), move on and seize another road a mile or more in my rear, which two roads were the only avenues in that neighborhood leading to James River. Had he succeeded in routing*

---

[68] OR, Volume XI, Part II, p 111

my division he would have accomplished his object, viz., to cut off Heintzelman, Franklin, and Kearny from the main body of the army."[69]

Afterwards Lee wrote:
"At the close of the struggle nearly the entire field remained in our possession, covered with the enemy's dead and wounded. Many prisoners, including a general of division, were captured, and several batteries, with some thousands of small-arms, taken. Could the other commands have cooperated in the action the result would have proved most disastrous to the enemy."[70]

In a letter dated November 25, 1862, from captured Union Surgeon Nathaniel Frederick Marsh, 4th Pennsylvania Cavalry in McCall's division (the letter was sent to McCall after both had been traded for Confederate prisoners), Marsh related a conversation he had with Confederate General James Longstreet on the day after Glendale. Longstreet asked which troops were engaged.

"I replied, I only knew the division I was connected with (McCall's), which fought just where we then were. General Longstreet said, 'Well, McCall is safe in Richmond; but if his division had not offered the stubborn resistance it did on this road we would have captured your whole army. Never mind; we will do it yet' ".

In his extensive memoirs written after the war, Confederate General Edward Porter Alexander pointedly wrote:
"Never, before or after, did the fates put such a prize within our reach. It is my individual belief that on two occasions in the four years, we were within reach of military successes so great that we might have hoped to end the war with our independence. ... The first was at Bull Run July, 1861 ... This chance of June 30, 1862 impresses me as the best of all."[71]

---

[69] OR, Vol. XI, Part 2, p 393

[70] OR, Vol. XI, Part 2, p 494

[71] Alexander, Edward P. *Fighting for the Confederacy: The Personal Recollections of General Edward Porter Alexander*. Edited by Gary W. Gallagher. Chapel Hill: University of North Carolina Press, 1989. ISBN 0-8078-4722-4.

By the end of the Seven Days, McCall's 3rd Division of the Pennsylvania Reserves would remain the hardest hit of all the Union Divisions. *"Echoes of Thunder: A Guide to the Seven Days Battles"* provides the following description:

"The night of June 30 found McCall's Division wrecked. It had fought three battles in five days, the most severe being at Glendale. During those three battles it had sustained 3067 killed, wounded and missing. This was a casualty rate of 30 percent. In addition to this high number of casualties, the command structure had been decimated. The division commander was captured, one brigade commander had been captured and his replacement killed, and one brigade commander had been wounded. The surviving brigade commander commanded the division, and the senior regimental commander in each brigade commanded his brigade. Losses among regimental and company grade officers had been high. The five batteries of artillery supporting the division went into battle at Glendale with a total of twenty-four cannon. Fourteen of these guns were captured by the attacking Confederates, thereby rendering the artillery minimally effective in future action. As the division limped south toward Malvern Hill, the survivors could say they had given everything they had."[72]

Of the batteries which began the *Seven Days Battles* with Battery B, Battery A's Captain Easton was killed at Gaines's Farm, Captain Kern, of Battery G, who had fought shoulder to shoulder with Cooper's Battery B, was wounded, and Captain De Hart of Battery C, 5th U.S. Light Artillery, was mortally wounded and died soon after. Captain Kern was still fighting side by side with Cooper when he was killed two months later, at *Second Bull Run* on August 30, 1862 – standing alone at his battery, single-handedly loading and firing until he was shot in a charge by Hood's Texas Brigade. Kern refused all aid from his captors, saying before he died, *"I have promised to drive you back or die under my guns, and I have kept my word."*

---

[72] *"Echoes of Thunder: A Guide to the Seven Days Battles"*, Matt Spruill III, Matt Spruill IV, 2006, University of Tennessee Press, Knoxville, 2006, p196-198

To: Capt. JAMES C. CLARK, Assistant Adjutant- General

Official Report of Capt. James H. Cooper, Battery B, First Light Artillery, of the *Battle of Glendale*:

The battery having been ordered by General McCall to take position in line of battle near the above-named place at 2 o'clock p.m., where we remained until 4.30 p. m., when one of the enemy's batteries, concealed in the woods to our front, opened fire upon us, to which we replied with marked effect, as soon but one gun replied to us. During the engagement parties of infantry attempted to cross the field in our front, but with the assistance of Battery G, First Pennsylvania Artillery, we compelled them to retire in disorder and confusion. This continued about one and a half hours, when Battery G was compelled to retire for want of ammunition, and our infantry support, with the exception of three companies, retired. The enemy, availing themselves of this opportunity, advanced a regiment from a point of woods in our front, which our canister failed to check, although it did marked execution. The remaining infantry falling back, we were compelled to retire from our guns. The charge being so sudden and overpowering it was impossible to remove them, many of the horses being killed by the enemy's fire. I hereby desire to bear testimony of the coolness and bravery of both men and officers in my battery during the three days engagement herein recorded.

Respectfully, your humble servant,
J. H. COOPER,
Captain, Pennsylvania Artillery, Comdg. Battery B.[73]

An 1864 engraving of the fight for McCall's artillery at Glendale

---

[73] OR, Volume XI, Part 2, pp. 410 - 411

White Oak Swamp in 2013 and (below) White Oak Swamp Bridge: destroyed by Union troops to delay the Confederate pursuit.

Map next two pages:
Map of the *Battle of Glendale*, showing the Pennsylvania Reserves artillery positioned to face the brunt of the attack from Longstreet and Hill. Adapted from a map made for Major General Heintzelman, III Corps, by R. K. Sneden, July, 1862. Library of Congress.

DAVID BUTT

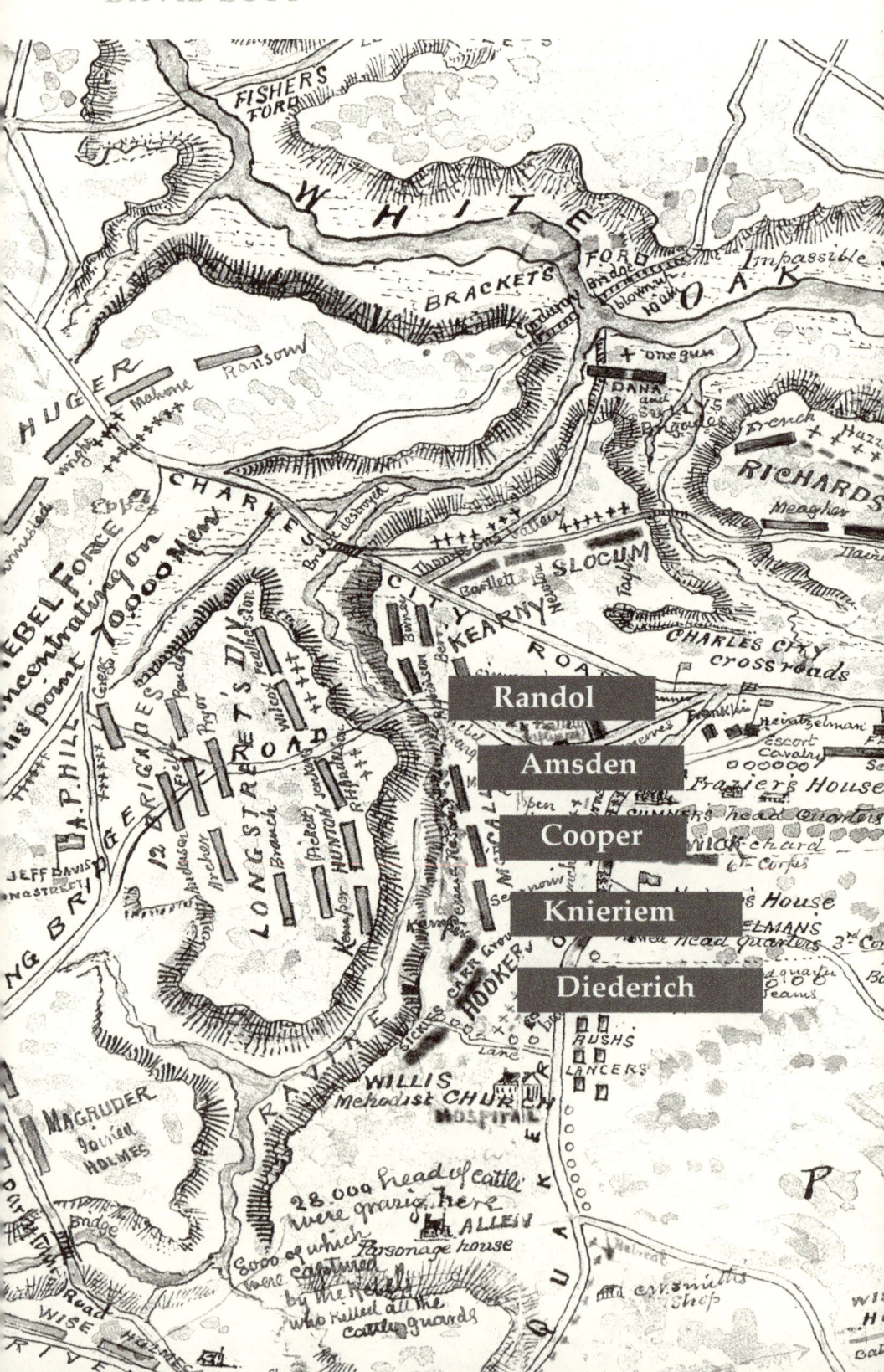

DAY 7: TUESDAY JULY 1
Battle of Malvern Hill

By Day 7, the entire Army of the Potomac had withdrawn to Malvern Hill, close to Harrison's Landing on the James River. And here they were in a highly favorable position which could be easily defended. Porter's V Corps, minus McCall's Division, had arrived the day before and had established a virtually impregnable defense from the vantage points on the hill down and across the areas over which the Confederates would need to attack – gently sloping and highly exposed ground.

As Lee prepared for the assault, McClellan's new Chief of Artillery, Colonel Henry J. Hunt (left), unleashed a 90 minute barrage from the 250 guns placed along the hill, as well as from three gunboats on the James River. Once again, poor command and communication resulted in a fragmented attack by the Confederates, with some twenty separate infantry brigades advancing across the open ground at different times: Confederate General D. P. Hill later wrote, *"It was not war – it was murder."*

The Confederates made repeated charges up the hill, but all for absolutely no gain. Lee's army suffered 5,650 casualties compared with 2,214 Union casualties. Such was the authority of the artillery that day that less than a third of the Union infantry took part in the battle. It was a pointless battle for the Confederates, and one which many of its generals questioned as their ranks marched headlong into withering fire.

Battery B reached Malvern Hill at sunrise on July 1 with other survivors from McCall's Pennsylvania Reserves Division, but with its guns gone did not take part in the battle. Harrison's Landing was reached the following day. Four guns, in place of those lost, were received on July 11. Throughout the Seven Days, Battery B had lost eight dead and mortally wounded, and another 11 wounded.

See illustration page 176.

THE END

The *Seven Days Battles* and the *Peninsula Campaign* were over.

The Union Army had suffered 15,855 casualties – 1,734 killed, 8,066 wounded and 6,055 missing or captured. The Confederate Army had suffered 20,204 casualties – 3,494 killed, 15,758 wounded and 952 missing or captured.

Yet in reality it was a disaster for the Union. All chances of victory were abandoned at the gates of Richmond and defeat had taken its place. The Union Army's opportunity to end the war had instead given new hope to the South, and brought further despair to the North. Lee had lost his first battle as Army Commander, but had been allowed to move on quickly from that defeat to sow the seeds of what became the story of a legendary commander. Richmond was safe for now, and conversely Washington and the North were not. Confident in his understanding of the way McClellan's mind worked, Lee could now take the battle to the North.

At Harrison's Landing, McCall's Division was in ruin and the survivors such as Private Dunnan and his fellow soldiers in Battery B were exhausted, with many of them wounded or sick. They had endured days of intense fighting, and witnessed comrades and opponents falling all around them, torn apart by cannon fire, bullets, bayonets and bloody hand to hand fighting, or wounded and left behind to be captured or die. This was all done in days and nights spent marching, fighting, and attempting to snatch some moments of sleep in swamps, mud, and rain.

McClellan's troops also were highly demoralized: they had spent months preparing for an assault on Richmond which had never occurred, and then had retreated rapidly even after they had won or at least held their positions in most of the seven days of subsequent battles. Indeed the only real Federal loss in the seven days was at Gaines's Mill, and even that could have been turned into victory had McClellan not held back his troops but rather had sent his numerous reinforcements to support Porter, or indeed launched a counter attack on Richmond.

The muddy bogs of the Peninsula gave rise to many exotic diseases such as typhoid and malaria. So by the time Battery B reached Harrison's Landing on the James River, many of the men were ill and others were highly susceptible to disease.

And in reality Harrison's Landing was another swamp – a sea of mud, poorly drained, with poor drinking water and with the unsanitary situation deteriorating daily. Sweltering in the heat and humidity at the height of the Virginian summer, it was the perfect incubator for diseases borne by an abundance of mosquitoes and flies. Chickahominy fever became James River fever.

Harper's Weekly, of July 19, 1862, provides the following description of Harrison's Landing:

The large Berkeley mansion, and the two smaller houses adjoining, as well as several negro huts in the vicinity, are all occupied as hospitals. ....The rain has poured down in torrents all day today; the grounds around the house are one mass of mud, and in two hours after the house was opened the rich carpets in every room were covered with a thick layer of the sacred soil, which, being tramped and grimed into them, has completely ruined them. Upon these once elegant but now muddy carpets our wounded officers and soldiers are now lying closely crowded together. Two of the rooms down stairs are used for amputations, and in this department of surgery the surgeons have been busy all day. For the want of space the sick and those slightly wounded are made to go outside the house, there not being room enough inside for the severely wounded alone.

Surgeon Jonathan Letterman, Medical Director of the Army of the Potomac, noted in his official report:

"The army when it reached Harrisons Landing was greatly exhausted. The malaria from the borders of the Chickahominy and from the swamps throughout the Peninsula to which it had been so freely exposed now began to manifest its baneful effects upon the health of the men. In addition to this the troops, just previous to their arrival at this point, had been marching and fighting for seven days and nights in a country abounding in pestilential swamps and traversed by streams greatly swollen by the heavy rains, which made that region almost a Serbonian bog. The labors of the troops had been excessive, the excitement intense. They were called upon to subsist upon a scanty supply of food, and but little time even to prepare the meager allowance. They had little time for sleep, and even when the chance presented itself it was to lie in the rain

and mud, with the expectation of being called to arms at any moment. The marching and fighting in such a country, with such weather, with lack of food, want of rest, great excitement, and the depression necessarily consequent upon it, could not have other than the effect of greatly increasing the numbers of sick in the army after it reached Harrisons Landing...... The supplies had been exhausted almost entirely or had from necessity been abandoned; the hospital tents had been almost universally abandoned or destroyed..... from the most careful estimate which I could make in the absence of positive data the sickness amounted to at least twenty per cent..... The deadly malaria was now producing its full effects and together with the want of proper food and the exposure to the rains which had fallen so continuously, and the fatigues endured, was now being fully manifested in the prevalence of malarial fevers of a typhoid type, diarrheas, and scurvy."[74]

July at Harrison's Landing turned out to be the most costly month of the Peninsula Campaign in terms of deaths and casualties from disease. Almost 43,000 cases of illness were reported, and in late July, 1862 – a month after his final diary entry – Private Robert Smiley Dunnan became one of these casualties: dead of typhoid soon after his 28th birthday.

The date of his death is variously recorded as either July 27 or 29. An obituary published in the local Pennsylvanian newspaper, the *New Castle courant*, in 1862 states:

"On Sunday the 27th ult. of brain fever after six days illness, Mr. Robert Dunnan, of North Beaver township, in the 28th year of his age. The subject of this notice was a member of the Mount Jackson Guards in the First Pennsylvania Artillery – had passed through all the trials and hair breadth escapes in the six days engagement before Richmond. He was an excellent young man – brave and patriotic. At the time when his country was first considered in danger he volunteered in its defense and has now rendered up his life on the altar for his country. We can truly sympathize with his many relatives and friends."

According to the US Department of Veterans Affairs and the Records of Glendale National Cemetery, Richmond, Henrico County,

---

[74] OR, Vol. XI, Part 2, pp.210-212

Virginia, Private Robert Dunnan was first buried at Harrison's Landing. When Glendale National Cemetery was established on May 7, 1866, the initial interments were the remains of Union soldiers recovered from Malvern Hill, Glendale, Harrison's Landing and other areas in the vicinity. An inspector's report of July 26, 1871, notes a total of 1,189 interments, including 236 known and 953 unknown gravesites. Robert Dunnan's grave is marked as Plot A 66 at Glendale.

The Honor roll records that, throughout the war, Battery B lost 2 Officers and 19 Enlisted men killed and mortally wounded and 17 Enlisted men by disease – a total of 38. This was the highest casualty rate of any militia battery during the war.

Of the 78 men of the original Mt Jackson Guard who left Mount Jackson on June 8, 1861, for the train in Enon Valley, 15 died – eight of them either killed in battle or mortally wounded. One man was killed accidentally and the remaining six died from disease. Another 17 of them were wounded, some of them more than once. Four of those men were discharged because of the severity of their injuries, including the loss of limbs. A further eight were discharged because of illness. That meant that of the original 78, more than half of them had died, been wounded, or discharged due to ill health.

General William "Baldy" Smith with other Union officers near Malvern Hill at the end of the *Seven Days Battles* on the Virginia Peninsula, July, 1862

POSTSCRIPT

By the end of the war, 625,000 people were dead and hundreds of thousands more wounded – this out of a total population of less than 32 million people. Some 150 years later, this still makes up almost half of all American war casualties in the country's entire history. The Civil War resulted in 50% more deaths than occurred in World War II when 405,000 Americans died – and by then the population of the United States had grown by another 100 million.

World War II resulted in three deaths for every 1,000 Americans. The Civil War killed 20 of every 1,000 Americans. On average, in World War II, 416 Americans died every day. In the Civil War, 600 Americans died each day.

If the casualty rate of the Civil War were repeated in a war involving the US population 150 years later, six million people would die.

So why such high casualty rates in the Civil War? There were four main reasons:

- *First*, while the machinery of war was rapidly being modernized, the tactics of war were not. Thus regiments of men would stand shoulder to shoulder – elbows touching – and march Napoleonic style into volleys of accurate musketry and the mouths of rifled cannon able to cut them down in swathes from a great distance or tear them apart from close range with barrages of canister and double shot.
- *Second*, many died from what are now regarded as common, preventable and treatable diseases and infections – estimated at double the number killed or mortally wounded in battle.
- *Third*, the flesh tearing and bone shattering wounds created by increasingly evolving lethal projectiles would often result in subsequent deaths due to trauma. The soft lead cylindrical bullets of the time – most commonly the 0.58 caliber Minie ball – would expand when they struck their target and leave large gaping holes through bodies and bones. A shot to the stomach, chest or head was largely seen as a death sentence, and thus the amputation of limbs became the common operation for the Civil War surgeon. In the Federal Army alone, there were 30,000 amputations and many

of those who lost limbs subsequently died from infections. Antiseptic surgery was not introduced until 1865.
- *Fourth*, and very importantly, the measurement of casualties for World War II and other wars in which Americans have engaged do not include enemy deaths. In the Civil War, it was Americans fighting Americans, and the casualties from both sides were counted together – brothers in arms forever.

Wounded soldiers in hospital: the weapons of the day resulted in high rates of amputations and mortality

General John Sedgwick (seated right) with Colonels Albert V. Colburn and Delos B. Sackett at Harrison's Landing in July, 1862

APPENDIX A

THE AFTERMATH:
General George Brinton McClellan 1826 – 1885

With the failure of the Peninsula Campaign, George McClellan came in for considerable criticism, both for his very cautious tactics and for the passive role he played in the final two days of the *Seven Days Battles*. Where there was a strong view that if McClellan had pushed forward early when the opportunities presented, Richmond would have been taken and the war would have been shortened, instead the Union had been defeated and retreated back over the James River. Lee was on the ascendancy and for the first time it was possible to believe that the South might achieve its independence.

Lincoln reorganized and created the Army of Virginia under Major General John Pope, but when Pope was defeated at *Second Bull Run* (August 28-30, 1862) – the next major battle for Battery B – Lincoln reluctantly turned back to McClellan as the man who could resurrect his ailing eastern army and defend Washington. The appointment was hugely controversial but Lincoln told his secretary, John Hay, *"We must use what tools we have. There is no man in the Army who can man these fortifications and lick these troops of ours into shape half as well as he. If he can't fight himself, he excels in making others ready to fight."*

With the success at Bull Run, Robert E. Lee marched his army into Maryland in early September. In the *Battle of South Mountain* on September 14, McClellan's army was able to break through the defended passes that separated them from Lee, but they also gave Lee enough time to concentrate many of his men at Sharpsburg, Maryland.

The subsequent *Battle of Antietam* on September 17, 1862, remains the single bloodiest day in American military history. The outnumbered Confederate forces fought fiercely and well against McClellan's significantly larger army. Despite being a tactical draw, Antietam is considered a turning point of the war and a victory for the Union because it ended Lee's first invasion of the North and allowed Lincoln to issue the Emancipation Proclamation on September 22, taking effect on January 1, 1863. Although Lincoln had intended to issue the proclamation earlier, he was advised by his Cabinet to wait until a Union victory to avoid the perception that it was issued out of desperation.

When McClellan failed to pursue Lee aggressively after Antietam, Lincoln ordered that he be removed from command on November 5. Major General Ambrose Burnside assumed command of the Army of the Potomac on November 7.

Lincoln in McClellan's tent after the
Battle of Antietam.
It was the last time the two would meet.

As the war progressed, there were various calls to return McClellan to an important command, following the Union defeats at Fredericksburg and Chancellorsville, and as Lee moved north at the start of the Gettysburg Campaign. When Ulysses S. Grant became General-in-Chief, he also discussed returning McClellan to a senior position.

But all of these opportunities were impossible, given the opposition within the administration and the knowledge that McClellan posed a potential political threat. Then, in October, 1863, McClellan was nominated by the Democrats to run against Lincoln in the 1864 U.S. presidential election. Lincoln won the election easily, with a vote of 2,218,388 to 1,812,807 or 55% to 45%.

At the conclusion of the war, McClellan and his family moved to Europe (not returning until 1868). In 1877, McClellan was elected as Governor of New Jersey and served a single term from 1878 to 1881.

McClellan's final years were devoted to traveling and writing, including his memoirs, *McClellan's Own Story* (published posthumously in 1887), in which he vigorously defended his conduct during the war. He died of a heart attack at age 58 at Orange, New Jersey, after having suffered from chest pains for a few weeks. He was buried at Riverview Cemetery, Trenton, New Jersey.

The debate over McClellan's ability, talents and achievements has remained the subject of much controversy among Civil War and military historians ever since.

General George Archibald McCall   1802 – 1868

George McCall was recognized for the high standards of leadership and bravery which he displayed in the battering which his Pennsylvanian Reserves Division gave and received in the Seven Days Battles. Wounded and captured at Glendale, McCall was imprisoned in Libby Prison in Richmond, Virginia. Previous illness was aggravated by his confinement in prison, and after his exchange (for Confederate Brigadier General Simon Bolivar Buckner) in August, 1862, McCall went on extensive recuperation leave and ultimately resigned due to poor health in March, 1863.

In retirement, McCall farmed in Pennsylvania. He died at his "Belair" estate in West Chester, Pennsylvania, in February, 1868, aged 65 and was buried in Christ Church Cemetery in his native Philadelphia.

General George Gordon Meade   1815 – 1872

After being severely wounded in the arm, back, and side at Glendale on June 30, George Meade partially recovered his strength in time for the Northern Virginia Campaign and the *Second Battle of Bull Run* two months later. Meade's 1st Brigade was a part of the

DAVID BUTT

Pennsylvania Reserves Division then headed by Brigadier General John F. Reynolds and with a regiment of four artillery batteries including Battery B. They were at that time assigned to Major General Irvin McDowell's III Corps of the Army of Virginia. At Bull Run the Pennsylvania Reserves made a heroic stand on Henry House Hill which served to protect the rear of the retreating Union Army.

At the start of the Maryland Campaign a few days later, Meade received command of the 3rd Division, I Corps, Army of the Potomac, under Major General Joseph Hooker, with Battery B now a part of his artillery regiment.

As division commander he had notable success at the *Battle of South Mountain* and assumed temporary I Corps command at the *Battle of Antietam* when Hooker was wounded. Reynolds was absent for the *Battle of Antietam* but took over command of I Corps when Hooker was promoted to run a "Grand Division". Meade's 3rd Division of Pennsylvania Reserves, with its increasingly famous artillery, made one of the few successful assaults at the *Battle of Fredericksburg*, inflicting considerable casualties on Stonewall Jackson's troops, but the Union commanders failed to capitalize on the opportunity.

Just three days before the *Battle of Gettysburg*, Meade was appointed to command the Army of the Potomac. He had not actively sought command and was not President Lincoln's first choice. Reynolds, one of four major generals who outranked Meade in the Army of the Potomac, had earlier turned down the president's suggestion that he take over. However Meade was able to organize his forces to fight a successful defensive battle against Robert E. Lee and achieve victory in what is seen as one of the great turning points of the war.

In 1864–65, Meade continued to command the Army of the Potomac through the Overland Campaign, the Richmond-Petersburg Campaign, and the Appomattox Campaign, but this was done in the shadows of the General-in-Chief, Lieutenant General Ulysses S. Grant, who accompanied him throughout those campaigns.

After the war Meade commanded several important departments during Reconstruction. While still on active duty, George Meade died in Philadelphia from complications of his old wounds, combined with pneumonia, on November 6, 1872. He was buried in Laurel Hill Cemetery.

General George Meade and staff

General John Fulton Reynolds 1820 – 1863

After he was captured at Gaines's Mill on June 27, John Reynolds was transported to Richmond and held at Libby Prison, but was quickly exchanged on August 15 (for Confederate Brigadier General Lloyd Tilghman).

Upon his return, Reynolds was given command of the Pennsylvania Reserves Division, in place of the captured McCall. The Pennsylvania Reserves was one of three Divisions in Major General Irvin McDowell's III Corps which joined the Army of Virginia under Major General John Pope at Manassas in late August, 1862. The Reserves were made up of three brigades headed by Generals Meade, Seymour, and newly appointed Brigadier General C. Feger Jackson (previously Colonel in charge of the 9th Regiment, Pennsylvania Reserves, and the officer who led the charge which recaptured Cooper's guns at the *Battle of Glendale* on June 30). His command also included a regiment of four artillery batteries including Cooper's Battery B.

On the second day of the *Second Battle of Bull Run*, while most of the Union Army was retreating, Reynolds led his men in a last-ditch stand on Henry House Hill, site of the great Union debacle at *First Bull Run* the previous year. Waving the flag of the 2nd Reserves regiment, he yelled, *"Now boys, give them the steel, charge bayonets, double quick!"* His counterattack halted the Confederate advance long enough to give the Union Army time to retreat in a more orderly fashion, arguably the most important factor in preventing a repeat of the previous year's debacle.

At the request of Pennsylvania Governor Andrew G. Curtin, Reynolds was then given command of the Pennsylvania Militia during General Robert E. Lee's invasion of Maryland. Reynolds spent two weeks in Pennsylvania drilling the local militia and missed the *Battle of Antietam*. However, he returned to the Army of the Potomac in late 1862 and assumed command of I Corps from Major General Hooker who had been promoted to command a "Grand Division" made up of two Corps. One of Reynolds's divisions, commanded by General Meade and supported by Battery B, made the only breakthrough at the *Battle of Fredericksburg*. After the battle, Reynolds was promoted to major general of volunteers, with a date of rank of November 29, 1862.

Because of problems with communications and organisation, the 17,000 troops in Reynolds's I Corps had little involvement in the Union loss at the *Battle of Chancellorsville* in May, 1863. Reynolds clashed with Major General Hooker, by this time the commander of the Army of the Potomac, over what he regarded as poor decisions in the battle and joined several of his fellow officers in urging that Hooker be replaced. Reynolds had taken a similar approach when he had spoken out against then Commander of the Army of the Potomac Major General Ambrose Burnside after Fredericksburg.

On June 2, 1863, President Lincoln met privately with Reynolds and is believed to have asked him whether he would consider being the next Commander of the Army of the Potomac. Reynolds supposedly replied that he would be willing to accept only if he were given a free hand and could be isolated from the political influences that had affected the Army commanders throughout the war. Unable to agree, Lincoln promoted the more junior General Meade to replace Hooker on June 28.

At what became the *Battle of Gettysburg*, on the morning of July 1, 1863, Reynolds was commanding the "left wing" of the Army of the Potomac, with operational control over the I, III, and XI Corps, and Brigadier General John Buford's cavalry division. As Union and Confederate forces began to engage near the town, Reynolds rode out to meet with Buford, and then accompanied some of his soldiers into the fighting at Herbst's Woods. Troops began arriving from Union Brigadier General Solomon Meredith's Iron Brigade, and as Reynolds was supervising the placement of the 2nd Wisconsin, he yelled at them, *"Forward men! For God's sake forward!"* At that moment he fell from his horse with a wound in the back of the upper neck, or lower head, and died almost instantly.

For the Union side, the death of John Reynolds was a major blow as he was highly regarded as both an inspirational and astute leader.

Reynolds's body was taken to his birthplace, Lancaster, Pennsylvania, where he was buried on July 4, 1863.

"The Fall of Reynolds" by Alfred Waud
drawing of Reynolds's death at Gettysburg

Captain James Harvey Cooper 1840 - 1906

James Harvey Cooper was born on March 6, 1840, in Allegany County, Pa, and, along with the Dunnan brothers, enlisted in the Mt Jackson Reserves on April 26, 1861. He was immediately elected

DAVID BUTT

Sergeant, entered the State service on June 8, and was then elected Second Lieutenant on the date that Battery B was mustered in – June 28. On August 2, 1861, after the Battery's first Captain, Henry Danforth, was promoted to Colonel and transferred (against his wishes), Cooper was promoted to the rank of Captain and placed in charge of Battery B – a position he fulfilled bravely for the next three stormy years.

By the end of the *Seven Days Battles*, Cooper's Battery had lost eight dead or mortally wounded and another 11 wounded, some with loss of limbs. Four guns to replace those lost were received at Harrison's Landing on July 11. On August 15, Battery B departed to join the Pennsylvania Reserves Division under the command of Major General Reynolds in Major General Irvin McDowell's III Corps which joined the Army of Virginia at Manassas in late August, 1862.

On day two of the *Second Battle of Bull Run* (August 30, 1862), Battery B played an important role in the counterattack led by Reynolds and Meade which halted the Confederate advance and enabled the Union Army to make an orderly retreat, thus avoiding another wholesale rout as occurred at *First Bull Run*.

At the *Battle of Fredericksburg*, (December 13, 1862) Battery B again played a critical role. Under cover of Battery B's guns, General Meade made a successful charge, and considerable damage was done to Stonewall Jackson's opposing artillery by the Battery's fire. Then the tide of battle turned, and the Union forces were driven back, the Southern forces following closely after them. Battery B maintained its position when all other artillery had retreated, keeping up a furious fire of double canister charges, and, supported by the infantry of the 37th New York, held the Union line. Jackson's forces came within 50 yards of Battery B before they finally broke and retreated under withering fire. It was on the occasion of this defense that General Reynolds cried out from on horseback nearby, *"Captain Cooper, you are the bravest man in the army"*.

Cooper's Battery fought in many more of the most significant battles of the war, including Antietam, Gettysburg (where in early July, 1863, the unit suffered three battle deaths but helped repel the famous attack known as "Pickett's Charge"), Spotsylvania, and Cold Harbour. Battery B was taking part in the Siege of Petersburg when the Confederate forces surrendered on April 9, 1865.

Twice Cooper had his horse killed beneath him – on one occasion at the *Battle of Antietam* his horse was blown apart by a solid cannon ball shot. But throughout the war Cooper continued to show courage and coolness under fire, and held his ground against the odds – an inspiration to his men and to those around them.

On August 5, 1864, General Meade and General Henry Hunt, the Chief of Artillery for the Army of the Potomac who had served closely with Cooper, and Colonel Charles S. Wainwright, who commanded Cooper as head of the I Corps Artillery Brigade at Gettysburg, recommended Cooper to fill a vacant colonel position, but Cooper never presented the petition to the War Office. He also had declined Pennsylvania Governor Andrew Curtin's offer of a major's commission in June that year.

Having remained two months beyond his term of service, Captain Cooper was mustered out on August 8, 1864, at his own request. He was belatedly commissioned as Major on September 24, 1864. But in subsequent public events – for example, at reunions of the *Association of Battery B* in which he retained a very active role – he maintained his title as Captain.

Cooper was replaced by Lieutenant William C. Miller, one of the early recruits to the battery, who had been wounded at Bull Run on August 29, 1862 and again at Gettysburg on July 2, 1863. When Miller was honorably discharged on November 22, 1864, Lieutenant William McClelland, an original member of the Mt Jackson Guards, was appointed commander and promoted to captain on February 23, 1865.

Captain McClelland turned Battery B in at Washington on June 3, 1865, and the troops were mustered out at Harrisburg on June 9. The Battery's normal strength was from 100-152 men, with numbers depending on when it had four or six guns. Over the four years of service, 334 men were connected with the battery and more than 11,200 rounds of ammunition were fired. The battery lost 21 men killed and mortally wounded – the greatest loss of any volunteer battery during the war – and 17 men by disease. There were 52 men wounded but many were wounded more than once, making the total wounded 101, although Cooper never allowed those with minor wounds to be counted as wounded.

As an original command, Battery B was the only part of the Pennsylvania Reserve Corps which served with the Army of the Potomac for the entire war. The Battery fought in twenty-seven of the principal engagements of the Army of the Potomac, and in nine of the twelve major battles of the entire war.

After the war, Cooper returned to New Castle and operated a lumber business known as Hammond & Cooper. He also was a part of the merchant tailoring firm of Cooper & Butler which operated on the main street of New Castle and dealt in men's clothing. He served as Sheriff of Lawrence County from 1874 to 1876.

In the summer of 1905, while Cooper was attending the National Encampment of the Grand Army of the Republic in Denver, Colorado, he became ill and was discovered to have a heart condition. He returned home and recovered to some extent but then went into decline and died in March, 1906, soon after his 66th birthday. He was buried at Greenwood Cemetery, New Castle.

"Cooper's Arty" – men from Battery B relaxing behind their artillery – drawn in pencil by famed Civil War artist Alfred R. Waud between 1861 and 1863. [75]

---

[75] From the 1919 J.P. Morgan collection of Civil War drawings, gifted to the Library of Congress. http://www.loc.gov/pictures/item/2004660100/

The Dunnan Soldiers:

Samuel Dunnan (1832-1922) was promoted from Corporal to Sergeant on November 1, 1862; and to Quarter Master Sergeant on June 28, 1864. He was mustered out with the battery on June 9, 1865. He married Lavira A. Covert in 1868 and they had four children, all born in Leetonia, near Salem, in Columbiana County, Ohio.

The Minutes of the twenty-second Annual Reunion of the Association of Battery B, held at Mt Jackson on June 8, 1891, record Samuel Dunnan as being present and register his address as New Lisbon (near Leetonia) in Ohio. At that time, Captain Cooper was President of the Association.

Lavira died in 1912 and Samuel died in Lisbon, Ohio, on 8 July, 1922, at the age of 90.

John Dunnan (1842-1923) was mustered out on June 9, 1864, at the expiration of his three-year term and returned to the family farm. He married Mary Ellen Martin in 1878 and they had three children: Bessie Lunetta Dunnan, Ruth Ann Dunnan, and James Martin Dunnan, all born in North Beaver Township. John Dunnan's wife, Mary Ellen, died in 1887 when the children were still very young, and in 1891 he married Harriet J Lusk. They had no children.

The Minutes of the Annual Reunion of Battery B of June 8, 1891, record John Dunnan as being present and register his address as Mt Jackson, Lawrence County. The Minutes also record John Dunnan as being an active participant in the Association as he was appointed to the Board of Directors.

John Dunnan sold his farm in 1905 and bought the Woodburn store at Mt. Jackson, which he operated with his son, James Dunnan. He died at Mt Jackson in 1923 aged 80. Harriet died in 1929.

James Dunnan (1830-1904) enlisted in Company G of the 3rd Iowa Cavalry Volunteers at Keosauqua, on August 26, 1861, as First Corporal. James is recorded as being from Keosauqua but as a native of Pennsylvania. He was mustered in at Keokuk, Iowa, on August 30, 1861, promoted to Fifth Sergeant on November 9, 1862, and Fourth Sergeant on January 1, 1864.

Company G was a part of the 2nd Battalion of the Regiment and saw service in Northern and Southern Missouri, largely against Confederate guerillas. The company also was a part of the campaign against Little Rock, Arkansas, and later saw service in Memphis, Tennessee.

On February 1, 1864, James was one of more than 600 men in the regiment who re-enlisted for another three year term. A month long furlough was granted to the regiment's re-enlisting veterans with transportation provided to Keokuk, Iowa, and James took that opportunity to marry Rachel Alcorn (1830-1904) at Lowell, Ohio, near the Pennsylvania border.

After returning to the regiment, James was promoted to Third Sergeant on December 1, 1864, and Company Commissary Sergeant on December 21, 1864.

The Regiment was mustered out on August 9, 1865, at Atlanta, Georgia, and the soldiers were given a train ride to Davenport, Iowa. On their arrival, the people of Davenport gave them a heroes' welcome. They then disbanded and returned to their homes.

Of the 2,165 men who served in the Regiment during the war, the regiment lost five Officers and 79 Enlisted men killed and mortally wounded and four Officers and 230 Enlisted men by disease – a total of 318.[76]

After the war, James and Rachel lived in Ohio and had three children – John Dunnan, Mary Elizabeth Dunnan, and Grace Dunnan. In 1890 they moved to Des Moines Township in Van Buren County, Iowa. Rachel died in 1904 and James died the following year at Mt Sterling in Van Buren County.

Hugh Dunnan (1839-1909) enlisted in the 5th Regiment, Pennsylvania Heavy Artillery (204th Volunteers) which was organized at Pittsburgh in August and September, 1864. Ironically – or perhaps on purpose given what his brothers had done – Hugh served in the 5th's Battery B.

The Regiment was ordered to Washington in September, 1864, attached to the District of Alexandria, 22nd Corps, to November,

---

[76] http://www.civilwararchive.com/Unreghst/uniacav.htm#3rdcav

BATTERY B

1864, and then to the 1st Separate Brigade, 22nd Corps, to June, 1865, when it was mustered out.

The Regiment served in the Northern Defenses of Washington and along Manassas Gap Railroad, protecting supplies for Major General Phillip Sheridan, and constantly engaged with the guerilla raids led by Confederate Colonel John Singleton Mosby. They were involved in action at Salem on October 4, 1864, Rectortown on October 7, and White Plains on October 11. Their duty on the Bull Run battlefield near Manassas in the spring of 1865 involved burying nearly 2,000 dead. They were ordered to Pittsburgh and mustered out on June 30, 1865. The Regiment lost three Enlisted men killed and 46 by disease.

In 1876, Hugh married Elizabeth (Eliza) Jennings Wallace (1852-1924) and the couple had five children – James Wallace Dunnan (1877-1944), Margaret Emma Dunnan (1879-1957?), Anna Jeanette Dunnan (1882-1949), Martha Minnie Dunnan (1893-1893), and Luella Eliza Dunnan (1890-1951). The family lived at North Beaver Township in Lawrence County, Pa., but by 1900 Hugh and Eliza had moved to Patton Township in Ford County, Illinois. Hugh died in Ford County in 1909 and Eliza died in 1924.

The family tree of John and Ann Smiley Dunnan can be found at: http://familytreemaker.genealogy.com/users/m/c/c/Dana-J-Mccown-Toowoomba/ODT1-0001.html

Pontoon bridge across the James River

APPENDIX B

RETURN OF ROBERT DUNNAN'S DIARY AND REVOLVER

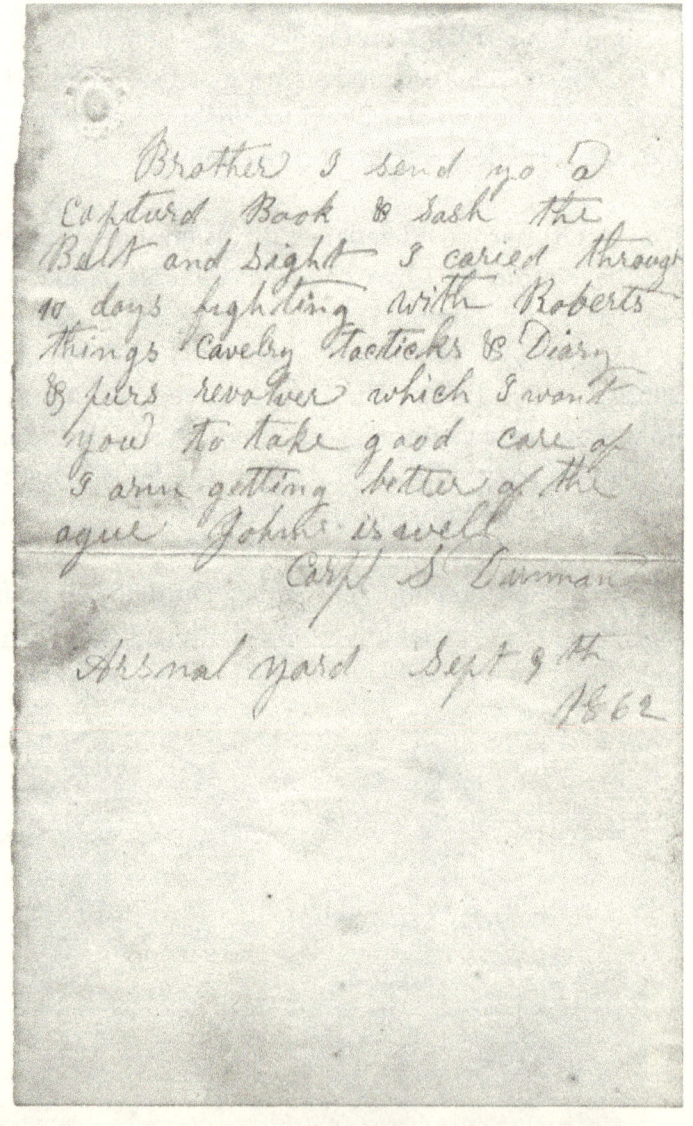

Letter from Sgt. Samuel Dunnan to Hugh Dunnan, September 9, 1862, accompanying Robert Dunnan's diary and revolver. The letter was kept with the diary.

APPENDIX C

OFFICIAL ARMY RECORDS

```
Dunnan, Robert S        B - 1 A            1 - 979
Enrolled 6-8-61                    At Harrisburg, Pa.
M.I. 6-28-61   As Pvt.             At Camp Wright
M.O.
Discharged
Age at enrollment 23               Complexion, Dark
Height 5'10                        Eyes, Blue
Hair, Dark                         Occupation, Carpenter
Residence, Mt. Jackson, Pa.
Remarks. Died 7-29-62 (at Harrison's Landing, Va. Bates)
```

```
Dunnan, Samuel          B - 1 A            1 - 977
Enrolled 6-8-61                    At Harrisburg, Pa.
M.I. 6-28-61   As Pvt.             At Camp Wright
M.O. 6-9-65
Discharged
Age at enrollment 25               Complexion, Dark
Height 5'8½"                       Eyes, Blue
Hair, Black                        Occupation, Carpenter
Residence, Mt. Jackson, Pa.
Remarks. (Pr. Corp. 8-2-61. Sgt. 11-1-62. Bates). Re-
enlisted 1-4-64. (Pr. Q.M. Sgt. 6-28-64. Bates).
```

```
Dunnan, John            B - 1 A            1 - 979
Enrolled 6-8-61                    At Harrisburg, Pa.
M.I. 6-28-61   As Pvt.             At Camp Wright
M.O.
Discharged 6-9-64
Age at enrollment 19               Complexion, Light
Height 5'9."                       Eyes, Blue
Hair, Dark                         Occupation, Farmer
Residence, Mt. Jackson, Pa.
Remarks. Disc. exp. of term.
```

Official Army records from the Pennsylvania State Archives

APPENDIX D

BATTERY B – RECORD OF ENGAGEMENTS 1861-1865

Dranesville ~ December 20, 1861

Beaver Dam Creek/Mechanicsville ~ June 26, 1862

Gaines's Mill ~ June 27, 1862

Glendale ~ June 30, 1862

Malvern Hill ~ July 1, 1862

Gainesville ~ August 28, 1862

Groveton ~ August 29, 1862

Second Bull Run ~ August 30, 1862

South Mountain ~ September 14, 1862

Antietam ~ September 16-17, 1862

Fredericksburg ~ December 13, 1862

Fitzhugh's Crossing ~ April 30, 1863

Chancellorsville ~ May 2, 1863

Gettysburg ~ July 1-3, 1863

Mile Run ~ November 27, 1863

Wilderness ~ May 5, 1864

Spotsylvania ~ May 12, 1864

North Anna River ~ May 23, 1864

Totopotomoy Creek ~ May 28, 1864

Bethesda Church ~ May 30, 1864

Cold Harbor ~ June 3, 1864

Petersburg ~ June 17, 1864

Weldon Railroad ~ August 18, 1864

Petersburg (capture) ~ April 2, 1865

Appomattox ~ April 9, 1865

Mustered out at Harrisburg, Pennsylvania, June 9, 1865, after four years' service

APPENDIX E

ROLL OF HONOR
Battery B: 43rd Regiment (1st Artillery)

- Thomas Cadwalader, Second Lieutenant, killed at Glendale, Va., June 30, 1862.
- Henry T. Danforth, Second Lieutenant, killed at Glendale, Va., June 30, 1862.
- James S. Miller, Sergeant, killed at Glendale, Va., June 30, 1862.
- John P. Monasmith, Sergeant, died at Philadelphia, October 4, 1864.
- Isaac J. Grubb, Sergeant, killed at Petersburg, Va., April 2, 1865.
- John M. Williams, Corporal, killed at Bull Run, Va., August 29, 1862.
- Andrew J. Gilkey, Corporal, killed at Petersburg, Va., April 2, 1865.
- John W. Summers, Corporal, died April 17, of wounds received at Petersburg, Va., April 2, 1865.
- Alexander P. Alcorn, Private, killed at Gettysburg, Pa., July 1, 1863.
- Robert Chambers, Private, died May 4, 1862.
- Henry Caton, Private, died March 5, 1865.
- Robert S. Dunnan, Private, died at Harrison's Landing, Va., July 29, 1862.
- Hernando J. Duff, Private, died May 7, 1862.
- Samuel Duff, Private, killed at Fredericksburg, Va., December 13, 1862.
- Charles B. Elwell, Private, died May 31, 1862; buried in Military Asylum cemetery, D.C.
- John G. Hughston, Private, died.
- Peter G. Hoagland, Private, killed at Gettysburg, Pa., July 2, 1863.

- Henry Howe, Private, died at Philadelphia, Pa., November 17, 1864.
- F. J. Holford, Private, died at Alexandria, February 25, 1865 – grave 3,024.
- Franklin Johnston, Private, died July 24, of wounds received at Glendale, Va., June 30, 1862.
- Haines J. Kerns, Private, died October 7, 1862.
- James H. McCleary, Private, killed at Gettysburg, Pa., July 2, 1863.
- James McGinnis, Private, died May 24, 1862.
- T. K. McClelland, Private, died September 13, of wounds received at Bull Run, Va., August 29, 1862; buried in Military Asylum cemetery, D. C.
- James M. McClurg, Private, died at Georgetown, D. C., September 29, 1861; buried in Military Asylum cemetery, D. C.
- David Might, Private, killed at Bull Run, Va., August 30, 1862.
- George Ralston, Private, died at Alexandria, Va., July 9, 1864.
- Eli Shaffer, Private, died at Smoketown, Md., December 13, 1862.
- William H. Shaffer, Private, killed at Bull Run, Va., August 29, 1862.
- Frederick B. Seifert, Private, killed by accident, October 14, 1861.
- Edward M. Smoot, Private, killed at Mechanicsville, Va., June 26, 1862.
- David B. Stoudt, Private, died at City Point, Va., December 17, 1864.
- David L. Shoff, Private, died November 21, 1864.
- Thomas W. Tait, Private, died July 4, of wounds received at Mechanicsville, Va., June 26, 1862.
- Isaac P. Wilson, Private, died August 24, 1862, of wounds, with loss of leg, received at Glendale, Va., June 30, 1862.
- William N. Waldron, Private, wounded at Glendale, Va., June 30, 1862, died, date unknown.

APPENDIX F

DEDICATION OF BATTERY B MONUMENT AT GETTYSBURG

This address by First Lieutenant James A. Gardner was given on September 11, 1889, at the dedication of the monument on Cemetery Hill which commemorates the positions and deeds at the Battle of Gettysburg of the First Pennsylvania Light Artillery, Cooper's Battery B.

Comrades: - By invitation of the Pennsylvania State Commission on Gettysburg Monuments, we have come from our distant homes to this, the Nation's shrine, to unite in the services dedicatory of the memorials erected here by our grand old Commonwealth to mark the positions of her patriotic sons upon this historic battlefield, where armed rebellion received the crushing blow.

Standing upon this sacred place (which marks our position in the second day's engagement), surrounded by innumerable blessings and a universal prosperity on every side, and looking back and over these twenty-six years since last here met, we are able to determine with satisfaction and accuracy the value of our work.

To you, who left your homes and stood up as a mighty wall of defense between the misguided South and the loyal North, who so nobly fought upon the many bloody fields in Virginia, Maryland and Pennsylvania, for the preservation of the Union, the Constitution and the Laws, come this day the fruits of victories dearly won, and the proud recollections, the honors and the glories of duties well and faithfully performed.

This monument before you, was erected out of an appropriation made by this state, supplemented by some few individual contributions almost wholly given by members of our association. It marks one of the five positions occupied by this battery at the *Battle of Gettysburg,* and testifies not only to your valor, courage and heroism upon this memorable field; but by its approved inscriptions, will show something of the services of this organization during the war, to those who shall visit this historic spot in the years to come.

DAVID BUTT

And it was fitting that this memorial should be erected here in Pennsylvania, at Gettysburg, the high-water mark of the rebellion; upon this position where you were subjected to a most trying fire from the enemy, remained the longest, and had your greatest casualties; here where the Union troops fought with a supreme courage, and a determination to stay upon these lines and defeat the enemy.

On such an occasion as this, I can but briefly speak of the services of our organization: and following the recommendation of those who directed this memorial service, shall principally address you upon the work done by this battery at the *Battle of Gettysburg*.

Battery B, First Light Artillery, Pennsylvania Reserve Corps, was organized at Mount Jackson, Lawrence county, April 26, 1861, composed mainly of farmers' sons, business men and school teachers, all in the prime and vigor of manhood; from a locality unexcelled in thrift and in the intelligence and religious culture of its inhabitants. Henry T. Danforth, who served in Bragg's regular battery in the Mexican war, was its first captain, from which he was promoted to the lieutenant-colonelcy of the regiment. He was killed in action at Charles City Cross Roads, Virginia.

Our next captain was James H. Cooper, who commanded more than three years, till August 8, 1864, refusing all promotions. It was the judgment of this organization, and of those in high place in the army, that for bravery, coolness, deliberation and ability to command upon the battlefield, Captain Cooper had no superior, if indeed, he had an equal.

June 8, 1861, this command entered the State service, was formally mustered June 28, and was early in front of Washington, attached to General John F. Reynolds's First Brigade, of General George A. McCall's Division of Pennsylvania Reserves, with which it was at the *Battle of Dranesville* (December 20, 1861) where was achieved the first victory for the Army of the Potomac. As part of General Irvin McDowell's First Corps we advanced to Fredericksburg, Virginia, and from there were taken to the Peninsula and united to General Fitz John Porter's Fifth Provisional Corps.

With the Pennsylvania Reserves, we opened the *Seven Days Battles* at Mechanicsville (June 26, 1862), by firing the first artillery shot from the Union lines; with four guns to the right of the Bethesda Church road, and two at Ellerson's Mill, we successfully contested with McIntosh's, Johnson's and Braxton's batteries, and repelled charge after charge made by the brigades of Archer, Anderson, Pender, Field and Ripley. Our firing was fast, accurate and fatal; by it the enemy were terribly slaughtered - the greatest comparative loss to the enemy, during the war; the Union loss, three hundred and sixty-one; the Confederates between three and four thousand!

Next day at Gaines' Mill, "the Valley of the Shadow of Death", one of the best fought battles of the war, this battery to the right of the Watts house, beat and kept back the pressing lines of the enemy till darkness threw its shades around us, when we withdrew from the last line of battle, section by section.

At Charles City Cross Roads, or Glendale (June 30, 1862), on the left of the L. Bridge (or New Market) road, being that part of McCall's line where occurred Longstreet's terrific onslaught, we repelled charge after charge, exhausting all our canisters, and met the last fatal crash with shells only, fixed with short cut fuses - standing, finally alone, without artillery or infantry supports. At Malvern Hill, we lay under the fire of the enemy, in full view of the disastrous repulse of Lee's army.

Abandoning the Peninsula, with the Pennsylvania Reserves then under General Reynolds, we were the first of the Army of the Potomac that came to the assistance of General John Pope.

At Gainesville (August 28, 1862), we engaged the right of Jackson's Corps. Next day at Groveton, our battery advanced to the attack of Jackson's right, and when coming into action we were met at grapeshot range, by two batteries of the enemy in front, and one upon our left flank. There poured upon us the hottest and most disastrous fire ever received by us during our entire term of service - four men killed and fifteen wounded, in about twenty minutes.

At *Second Bull Run* (August 30, 1862), by the Chinn house on the extreme left, we received the fatal stroke of Longstreet's Corps, meeting it with shell and canister, and repelling the charges until the infantry supports (Milroy's) on our left were flanked and driven. This compelled our withdrawal, wherein we narrowly escaped capture. At Chantilly we were in the line of battle; but of this there is no official report.

At South Mountain (September 14, 1862), with General Joseph Hooker's First Corps, we ascended the mountain slope, took position on a knoll, shelled and engaged the enemy until they were driven from our front. At Antietam, on the evening of September 16, we advanced with the skirmish line, and with the brave "Bucktails" opened the battle near the "East Wood."

Next morning and day we were in position on Poffenberger's ridge whereon were thirty guns. Here we shelled and engaged the enemy south of us, towards the Dunker Church, protected the Union right, and repulsed an effort made by the enemy during the afternoon.

At Fredericksburg (December 13, 1862), we were at the angle of the Union left, from which General Meade successfully made his charge, under cover of our guns. Our accurate fire here blew up several limber chests of Jackson's artillery stationed on the ridge west of Hamilton's Crossing. When the enemy had repulsed our attacking division and were exultingly following in force, the guns of this battery stood fast when others left, and belching forth most furiously double charges of canister, with the support of Thirty-seventh New York, we repulsed the enemy, maintained the integrity of the Union left, when to be driven at that time would have brought disaster to our army.

It was a moment of great danger, a most critical moment; this battery proved itself equal to and worthy of the occasion, and General Reynolds, who was with us at the time, complimented our commander for the noble defense he had made, saying "Captain Cooper, you are the bravest man in the army."

At Fitzhugh's Crossing (April 30, 1863), below Fredericksburg, we covered the advance of our First Corps; but the disaster at Chancellorsville took us there, where we moved to the front, and upon the reluctant retreat, we covered the withdrawal across United States Ford, shelling the enemy.

We now come to the march for Gettysburg. The First Corps arrived at Emmitsburg, Maryland, June 29, 1863, and we were placed in battery on the Fairfield road. The next day we advanced three or four miles north to the vicinity of Marsh creek, and were again placed in battery on the Fairfield road, supported by General Abner Doubleday's division of our corps.

BATTERY B

On the morning of July 1, with Doubleday's Division (then under General Thomas A. Rowley), we moved on the extreme left toward Fairfield, with videttes (mounted sentries) thrown out, while the other divisions of our corps marched directly for Gettysburg. With Colonel Chapman Biddle's Brigade of Doubleday's Division, we crossed Marsh creek at the White Bridge, which point afterward became the rear of Longstreet's line. Here we first heard the sound of artillery. Passing up the west bank of Willoughby run, we entered the Hagerstown (Fairfield) road, turned to the right and came to near the Seminary ridge.

Leaving the road, we moved to the left and forward, and came into battery on a crest, the east bank of Willoughby run, south of the McPherson wood (Reynolds's Grove) supported by Biddle's Brigade. This was 12 midday, and the situation at that time was: General Lysander Cutler's Brigade of General James S. Wadsworth's Division of our corps, north of Chambersburg (Cashtown) pike, and General Solomon Meredith's "Iron Brigade" of the same division, in the McPherson wood, south of the pike. These brigades had been successfully engaged with Archer's and Davis' brigades, Heth's Division, A. P. Hill's Corps, capturing General Archer and several hundred prisoners.

General John F. Reynolds, our able corps commander, had been killed; but knowledge of this fact was withheld from his troops.

As Doubleday's Division arrived, Colonel Roy Stone's Pennsylvania Brigade, being slightly in the advance of Biddle's, was sent to fill a gap between Cutler and Meredith, while Biddle's Brigade was placed, under cover, at the crest, to Meredith's left. In our first position, we engaged Pegram's artillery, then on Herr's ridge, firing upon the infantry and artillery on our right. Pegram's batteries immediately engaged us, but soon ceased firing. About 1 or 1.30 p.m., the enemy opened an enfilading fire upon our lines from batteries posted on Oak Hill near our extreme right.

By direction of Colonel Charles S. Wainwright, our chief of artillery, we were withdrawn from the crest, moved back into the meadow between the crest and the Seminary, at a point south of the (now) Springs Hotel road, and changed front to right so as to face the new enemy and sweep Oak Hill with our fire. The enemy's reinforcement was Rodes' Division of Ewell's Corps, then forming across Oak Ridge at right angles with our line. The enemy's artillery which enfiladed us, were the batteries of Carter and Fry, and their fire caused Cutler to withdraw his brigade back to the Seminary Ridge, Biddle to change front to right, and Stone to place two of his regiments along the Chambersburg pike facing northward.

These changes of Cutler and Stone made an angle through which this battery could fire with effect from its position in the meadow, and we immediately opened upon Carter's guns, keeping up a warm contest and an accurate fire until Rodes' infantry came in sight. Iverson's North Carolina Brigade was in the lead, and as it moved in our front and was wheeled to the left to strike General Henry Baxter's Brigade of General John C. Robinson's Division of our corps, and the brigade of Cutler, we poured into it a most galling and destructive front and flank fire of case shot. This was about 2.30 p.m. Iverson was repulsed, his brigade was nearly annihilated and much of it captured.

Following Iverson was Daniel's North Carolina Brigade of the same division, which passed Iverson's right and coming toward our front, upon Stone's troops; but the fire of our guns and the musketry from Stone's regiments, checked the enemy just north of the railroad cut.

While these conflicts were taking place, Hill's Corps was forming on the west side for an attack, and as such a movement would render our situation untenable, Colonel Wainwright ordered Captain Cooper, about 3 p.m., to take a good position at the Lutheran Theological Seminary, in front of the professor's house. Leaving the meadow we took position to the front and right of the Seminary, in rear of a barricade of rails thrown up earlier in the day.

For a short time we were not engaged, the enemy having ceased his attacks. After the repulse of Daniel's Brigade heretofore mentioned, the enemy stationed Brander's (Virginia) battery on a hill to the north of the railroad cut, on the east side of Willoughby run. When it opened, its shots came directly into our front, and to this fire of the enemy we very effectively replied. During this artillery contest, Davis' Brigade formed under cover, and in conjunction with Daniel's Brigade, from the north side of the railroad cut, made another attack upon Stone's position.

We again assisted Stone, and the attempt of the enemy at this time to dislodge our Pennsylvania troops utterly failed. While thus engaged with Brander's Battery and the enemy's infantry we were subjected to a cross fire from Fry's Battery on Oak Hill, Carter's Battery having gone to the east side of Oak Ridge to engage the troops of the Eleventh Corps.

This over, Heth's Division pressed our front and left. Brockenbrough's Virginia Brigade engaged the "Iron Brigade," and Pettigrew's Brigade of North Carolinians swept across Willoughby Run south of the McPherson wood and struck Biddle's Brigade, lapping its left a considerable distance. Biddle, after a sharp contest, was outflanked and his small brigade driven from the crest to the seminary. The One Hundred and Fifty-first Pennsylvania, however, under Lieutenant-Colonel George F. McFarland, which was on Biddle's right near the edge of the wood, remained until pressed back by the next line.

Pettigrew's Brigade in attempting further advance was met by fire from our guns and from those on our right, causing it to hastily fall back, excepting the Twenty-sixth North Carolina, which halted in the woods. Heth's Division had thus far failed to drive our lines; but Pender's Division of the same corps advanced and passing over Heth's, attacked us, Scales' Brigade of North Carolinians on the left, and McGowan's Brigade of South Carolinians under Colonel Perrin on the right, the former reaching the Chambersburg pike south into the McPherson wood and the latter being to the south of Scales' right.

These fresh troops pressed forward and our lines at the woods and crest were compelled to give way. Scales' Brigade as a first line coming over the crest and in descending the slope encountered a most terribly destructive and withering fire from our guns and from those of Captain G. T. Stevens, Fifth Maine, Lieutenant Wilbur's section, L, First New York, and part of Lieutenant James Stewart's battery, Fourth United States - in all fourteen pieces that poured out case shot, shell and canister, by which Scales was halted with heavy loss, his brigade thrown into confusion and broken up, and himself and every regimental officer of his command either killed or wounded.

By reason of its condition and confusion, Scales' Brigade advanced no further; but McGowan's Brigade on its right escaped much of the artillery fire and was consequently more fortunate. This brigade in its advance was supported by the Twenty-sixth North Carolina of

Pettigrew's Brigade, and as they came a galling case shot fire was thrown upon them from our guns.

Captain Cooper caused our immediate front at the barricade to be cleared of our infantry, and then bearing the guns slightly to the left, poured into Perrin's troops a most disastrous fire of double charges of canister. Our immediate supports and the infantry to our left in the grove, consisting of Meredith's and Biddle's brigades (Second and Seventh Wisconsin, Nineteenth Indiana, One hundred and fifty-first, One hundred and forty-second and One hundred and twenty-first Pennsylvania and Twentieth New York State Militia), at the same time fired deadly volleys of musketry.

The severity of this fire staggered and checked Perrin and almost annihilated the left of this brigade, his troops being wholly swept away from the front of our guns. Of all these attacking forces a single color-bearer only, with a bravery to be admired, reached the rail barricade in front of us. Finding that he could not cross our works, Perrin by a movement placed one of his regiments on the left of our barricade, and turned our position after 4 p.m.

At a most opportune time Lieutenant-Colonel Alfred B. McCalmont, of the One hundred and forty-second Pennsylvania, came to Captain Cooper and informed him that the infantry on the left had gone, and unless he immediately withdrew he would be captured. We were then still engaging the enemy; but upon this information we limbered to the rear, passed out on the north side of the seminary, narrowly escaping capture, the enemy being around both flanks.

Passing through Gettysburg the battery came to Cemetery Hill. Just prior to the driving of our lines Captain Cooper had ordered full limbers to the guns and had sent the caisson line to Cemetery Hill. The caissons crossed south of the town, and when first within view of the Taneytown road observed the retreat of the corps which had been on our right. The road was full of artillery and infantry, but the First Corps lines were yet on Seminary Ridge.

When this battery arrived on East Cemetery Hill, it was placed in position where we now stand, on the left of the First Corps artillery; after which, at the request of General Doubleday, then commanding our corps, Captain Cooper performed staff duty in assisting to establish and strengthen the Union lines; and when General Winfield

S. Hancock first arrived, he came to this spot and consulted with General Adelbert Ames and Captain Cooper.

During the first day's fight we expended four hundred rounds of ammunition; Private Alexander P. Alcorn was killed, Lieutenant William C. Miller and Privates John W. Phillips, John Pauly and Asabel Shafer were wounded. One gun was disabled by recoil, but was repaired that evening.

The losses in this day's fight were heavy on both sides. The First Corps were over six thousand men - two-thirds of its fighting force; but of these about two thousand were missing or taken prisoners. The losses of the enemy in killed and wounded were fully as severe. Heth says he lost two thousand and seven hundred in about twenty-five minutes. Scales' and McGowan's Brigades each lost about five hundred. The Twenty-sixth North Carolina of Pettigrew's Brigade went in with "over eight hundred strong," and came out with but two hundred and sixteen for duty; its entire loss at Gettysburg was eighty-six killed and five hundred and two wounded, total five hundred and eighty-eight, most of which loss was sustained during the first day's fight. Carter's Battery lost four killed and seven wounded before it left Oak Hill. The enemy had been so badly punished that he could not follow up his success.

A much greater loss, however, had fallen upon the Union army by the death of General Reynolds, our beloved corps commander, who was without doubt the ablest officer then with the Army of the Potomac, and greater by far than any place he had ever filled, the finest of gentlemen, and in all the army, without a peer. He had been our commander when we were in his brigade, in his division, and in his corps; we were always with him up to his dying hour, the only part of the Pennsylvania Reserves that remained under his command, and the only Pennsylvania battery with him in the first day's fight.

To us he was greatly endeared; his death caused deep gloom in this organization, and strong men shed tears. But his spirit fought with the First Corps on yonder side of town that day: Cutler's, Meredith's, Stone's, Biddle's, Baxter's and Paul's brigades, against Archer's, Davis', Brockenbrough's, Pettigrew's, McGowan's, Scales', Lane's, Thomas', Iverson's, Daniel's, Ramseur's, and O'Neal's brigades - six Union brigades against twelve of the enemy!

On the morning of July 2, the men of this battery finished the construction of these four lunettes, here on East Cemetery Hill. During the day, previous to 4 p.m., we fired occasional shots (scarcely exceeding twenty-five in all) at small bodies of the enemy's infantry and cavalry, which were maneuvering in the skirting of some timber about one mile distant. The enemy during the same time threw occasional shots into our left flank from his batteries on Seminary Ridge, killing and disabling some of our horses.

The enemy's fire was no doubt for the purpose of securing the range of this hill; for we now know that it was part of Lee's plan of battle that Ewell should attack these high grounds if opportunity were afforded. At 4 P.M. the terrible crash of the enemy's artillery came. Opposite this part of the Union line was Ewell's Corps, and in our immediate front was the division of General Edward Johnson.

On Benner's hill, directly opposite to us, were placed the batteries of Andrews' battalion under Major Latimer, consisting of the following in order from their right to their left: Brown's Maryland Battery of four 10-pounder Parrotts; Carpenter's Virginia Battery of two 3-inch rifle and two light 12-pounders; Dement's First Maryland of four light 12-pounders; two guns of Raine's Virginia Battery, one 10-pounder Parrott and one 3-inch rifle - in all eight rifle 10-pounders and six light 10-pounders - fourteen guns in all on Benner's hill, about twelve to fourteen hundred yards distant.

To the right of these batteries (our left) on the same ridge, beyond the Hanover road, about eighteen hundred yards distant, were posted Graham's Virginia Battery of four 20-pounder Parrotts, and two guns of Raine's Virginia Battery. Two 20-pounder Parrotts, the latter being between Graham and the guns of Latimer -- in all, six 20-pounder Parrotts.

To meet this fire we had from right to left Captain G. T. Stevens' Fifth Maine, six light 12-pounders (on the left slope of Culp's Hill); and Captain G. H. Reynolds' "L" First New York, five 3-inch rifle; Captain J. H. Cooper's "B" First Pennsylvania (this battery in this position) four 3-inch rifle; and Captain M. Wiedrich's "I" First New York, four 3-inch rifle (on East Cemetery Hill) - in all thirteen 3-inch rifle 10-pounders and six light 12-pounders.

At the hour named, 4 p.m., all these guns of the enemy opened upon us a most accurate fire. But this was not all. Ewell's chief of artillery had placed on Seminary Ridge, Dance's, Watson's and Smith's Virginia batteries, consisting of twelve 10-pounder rifled guns, which with other batteries on that ridge at the same time opened a flank fire upon this part of Cemetery Hill. The enemy's fire upon this position where we now stand was very severe. One of their shells struck and exploded at our No. 3 gun, killing and wounding every man at that place, but before the wounded were removed No. 3 gun was again at work, mention of which is made in Colonel Wainwright's official report.

The axle of our No. 2 gun was struck by a shell and broken; but the fire from this piece was also continued until the gun carriage broke down - this shortly before the contest closed. The shots of the enemy came thick and fast, bursting, crushing, and plowing, a mighty storm of iron hail, a most determined and terrible effort of the enemy to cripple and destroy the guns upon the hill.

Situated as we were in the center of this artillery fire, our battery received the full force of the enemy's front, oblique and flank fire. Against the batteries on Seminary Ridge we were powerless; but upon the batteries of Latimer on Benner's Hill, and upon Graham and Raine to our left, an accurate and most telling fire was opened from the batteries on this hill and continued for about two hours.

During about one-half hour of this time a part of Knap's Pennsylvania Battery, under Lieutenant Edward R. Geary, and a section of Battery K, Fifth United States Artillery, assisted us by a flank fire from Culp's Hill.

At last the batteries on Benner's Hill were forced to withdraw under our destructive fire, as their official report says, "by reason of the unequal contest, the overpowering of their artillery and the untenableness of the position." Brown was so badly used up that at the last he was able to use but two of his guns; and when he withdrew, his two right pieces were hauled off by hand. Shortly after Latimer's batteries had been withdrawn, one of them was brought back and posted to the left (our right); but upon it we brought additional guns and a concentrated fire, which very soon drove it away.

The losses of Andrews' Battalion on Benner's Hill were ten killed and forty wounded; among the latter was Major Latimer, the commander, who shortly afterward died of his wounds. Twenty-eight dead horses were left on the field, and the material of their batteries was very badly injured.

The losses in our battery were: Privates James H. McCleary and Peter G. Hoagland killed; Corporal Joseph Reed and Privates Jesse Temple, James C. Cornelius and Daniel W. Taylor wounded.

Soon after this artillery contest had ended, all our ammunition being exhausted, by order of Colonel Wainwright, we were relieved by Captain R. Bruce Ricketts' batteries "F" and "G" of the First Pennsylvania Artillery; but at what precise hour we will not determine. That the enemy opened at 4 p.m., is agreed to by all. Colonel Wainwright says the contest with the enemy's batteries on Benner's Hill lasted one and one-half hours; that the battery which afterward came out to our right was soon silenced, and that "soon after, Captain Cooper's Battery, which had suffered considerably, was relieved." Captain Cooper's official report says we were relieved about 7 p.m.

Of the enemy's reports, that of General Johnson says the contest lasted two hours, and that of Colonel Andrews (of Andrews' Battalion) says "till near night."

But the best evidence is our expenditure of ammunition. On that second day we fired about five hundred rounds, all we had, and more, for, at the last, we received a few rounds from an adjoining battery. About twenty-five rounds were used prior to 4 p.m., and about four hundred and seventy-five rounds after that hour, from four guns, three only at the last. The length of time required to expend such an amount of ammunition, will fix the time of our relief with reasonable accuracy.

Retiring from this position we passed down the Baltimore pike, and turned to the right, by a barn. The enemy's bullets came whistling in among us at that place, but the Twelfth Corps troops returning from the left, drove back the enemy. By order of Colonel Wainwright we proceeded to the camp of the Artillery Reserve, to refit, and refill with ammunition. By 11 a.m. of the next day our disabled gun was repaired and we were again ready for duty.

On July 3, at 1 p.m., when the enemy's one hundred and thirty-eight guns opened their great fire upon the eighty guns of the Union line between the Baltimore pike and Little Round Top, we were at the rear of our center; but shortly after the first burst of the enemy's

BATTERY B

artillery, General Henry J. Hunt, chief of artillery of the Army of the Potomac, ordered us to the front, to take position, and relieve a battery in Lieutenant Colonel Freeman McGilvery's line of Reserve Artillery, on the left center, the point reached being about one-half mile south of the clump of trees, and north of where the present railroad crosses Hancock avenue.

In coming to this position, we passed through a terrible fire at its height, cutting and slashing, and crashing against the rocks; the troops were hugging the ground, and sheltering behind earth, stone and everything and anything which would seem to give protection. The Union artillery, at this time, was replying to the enemy's fire.

We opened upon the enemy's line of batteries along the Emmitsburg Pike, firing but few shots until Captain Cooper received the order to cease firing. The entire Union line about the same time slackened and almost ceased its fire, for what purpose was, at the time, readily understood.

When Pickett's Division of Longstreet's Corps advanced under cover of artillery, in its now celebrated charge, its right flank received the destructive fire of our guns, until a battery of the Washington Artillery (Eshelman's) moved out some four hundred yards and opened upon the batteries and troops upon our right. Upon that battery our guns were immediately concentrated, completely shattering it and compelling its hasty withdrawal.

For about twenty to thirty minutes we ceased firing; but were soon confronted by Wilcox's Alabama Brigade, which was coming over the crest about 1,000 yards distant, moving directly toward us. Upon Wilcox's lines as they came, this battery in connection with adjacent batteries poured forth case shot until the enemy reached canister range, when double-charges were thrown into them with such telling effect that they were staggered, checked, routed and repulsed, without infantry assistance, leaving many dead and wounded in our battery front.

Of the enemy's wounded and surrendering troops, many were brought within the Union lines at our guns; and this virtually closed the *Battle of Gettysburg*. We expended this third day one hundred and fifty rounds of ammunition, and strangely escaped with but one casualty Private Frederick Workman, wounded.

At the beginning of this battle we had one hundred and fourteen officers and men "present for duty," of whom not over seventy-five to eighty were under fire at any one time. We expended in all 1,050 rounds of ammunition, about five tons. We had three killed and nine wounded; others were slightly injured, but Captain Cooper never reported any one as wounded who was able for duty.

In commemoration of this the greatest battle of the war, fought under the command of that accomplished soldier, the gallant and able General George G. Meade, a Pennsylvanian, and upon Pennsylvania soil, we have come to and do now dedicate this monument to the memory of our comrades who gave up their lives upon this hill, at the Seminary beyond and upon other fields; and as a testimonial to your valor in the dark days of this great Republic. Our other positions upon this field should yet be marked, especially the one at the Theological Seminary, and the one occupied in the third day's fight, at which it is hoped this association will yet erect suitable memorials.

Leaving victorious Gettysburg, we are next in line at Williamsport, Maryland, but not engaged; then in the game of "strategy" between Meade and Lee, along the Orange and Alexandria railway; then at Mine Run (November 27, 1863), where we warmly engaged the enemy on the Union left.

While the Army of the Potomac was in winter quarters near Culpeper, Virginia, the First Corps was consolidated with the Fifth Corps, under command of General G. K. Warren, a most excellent and worthy officer, with whom we ever afterward served.

On May 5, 1864, coming to the Wilderness with the Pennsylvania Reserves, we advanced to the Chewning farm near Parker's Store, then withdrew, narrowly escaping capture. Were next engaged at the Lacy house, and finally at the front line, on the Orange turnpike.

At Laurel Hill or Alsop's farm, we were hotly engaged, and being withdrawn, were hastily sent to the right and assisted the Second Corps in the repulse of the enemy at Po River. Returning from the Po, we were again placed close up to the enemy's line, where we treated the enemy to novel mortal practice from our guns.

By another left flank movement, we were in front of Spotsylvania Court House (May 12 to 18), where, in two positions, we engaged the enemy, in one of which they had upon us an accurate range and a raking fire. These three battles of Laurel Hill, Po River and Spotsylvania Court House, are designated by the War Department as "Spotsylvania," and as such is thus inscribed upon our monument.

At Jericho Ford, North Anna River, we next engaged the enemy, inflicting severe injury upon batteries on his right; after which we advanced with the front line. Moving forward we engaged the enemy at the Totopotomoy, at Bethesda Church, at bloody Cold Harbor, where we assisted in repulsing an attack upon the Fifth Corps lines; and finally we were in front of Petersburg (June 17, 1864), engaged in the assault of the outer lines, which were carried.

From the lines in front of Petersburg, where we had been constantly in action, we were next at the capture and defense of the Weldon railroad, at which, on both occasions, we were heavily and closely engaged with the enemy.

Having participated in the siege of Petersburg until the final attack came, early in the morning of April 2, 1865, we opened from our four guns in Fort Davis and from our two guns in Battery 22, a most accurate, vigorous and constant fire upon Fort Mahone ("Damnation") and the enemy's lines to right (Rives' salient), until the works on the right were captured; after which we directed our fire on Fort Mahone and the works immediately adjacent. During the forenoon of that day, Captain William McClelland, who was in command (Captain Cooper having been previously mustered out), with Lieutenant Thomas C. Rice and two detachments from the guns in Fort Davis, went to the recently captured part of the enemy's line, crossed over into their battery No. 27, and, under a hot fire, turned upon the enemy their own guns of Captain Patterson's Georgia battery of the Sumter artillery, and fired, of their own ammunition, six hundred rounds.

The remaining available section in Fort Davis was taken during the day to Fort Sedgwick ("Hell"), where it continued its fire. This was the last great battle in which we participated, and Captain McClelland, by his bravery, courage and ability, proved himself a most worthy and fitting successor to his illustrious predecessor in command. Our last loss was here - two killed, one mortally wounded and one officer and one non-commissioned officer slightly wounded; and with the race to Appomattox the record is closed. Turning in our guns and munitions of war, we were mustered out at Harrisburg, Pennsylvania, June 9, 1865, after full four years' service.

During our term, this battery fought in twenty-seven of the principal engagements of the Army of the Potomac (including Chantilly, Laurel Hill and Po River); and of twelve of the greatest battles of the war, wherein the Union losses in each were from eleven to twenty-three thousand, we were actively engaged in nine of them.

As a part of the Pennsylvania Reserve Corps, we were with the division longer than any other battery of our regiment, having served and fought with that organization during its entire existence, excepting, however, in the battles of Gettysburg and Mine Run, in which we were with the First Corps. And as an original command, we were the only part of the Reserves that served in the Army of the Potomac throughout till the close of the war.

The strength of the battery was one hundred to one hundred and fifty-two, a four gun or a six gun battery, according as we had men. Our total enrollment shows three hundred and thirty-two officers and men; but this includes two different details from the infantry, and a temporary transfer of some recruits, many of whom were finally sent to another battery of our regiment.

Our total expenditure of ammunition was over 11,200 rounds, or about fifty-six tons. We were always at the front, never in the rear; long range or short range, it made no difference, for we excelled in the accuracy of our fire and our shots counted, mention of which is made in the official reports.

Our total casualties were: Twenty-one (21) killed and died of wounds (two officers and nineteen men), seventeen (17) died of disease, etc.; and fifty-two (52) wounded (the latter not including our mortally nor those slightly injured). Our percentage of loss is smaller than that of many infantry companies; but this difference in percentage is not so much because of our less exposure to the enemy, but more by reason of a difference in methods of work on the field, and of our having had in action, at any one time, but two-thirds to three-fourths of those "present for duty."

Our loss in killed and died of wounds as it is, stands the greatest loss sustained by any volunteer battery of light artillery in the Union army, which is readily accounted for by our participation in the many principal engagements.

This hour and occasion permits only this brief reference to the service of our organization. I have aimed at accuracy, have given no glowing account, nor have I unduly magnified our work upon the field of battle. The official record will speak for us, and will furnish to faithful historians that which, when examined, will show that for length of term and active service in the field, principal engagements, ammunition expended and losses, we stand among the first, if not the very first, of all the batteries that fought in the Union cause.

And now, comrades, a word in conclusion. Having returned to our peaceful pursuits of life, we look back to the time when, upon this field and elsewhere, you were among the foremost men of this Nation; and right glad the people were then to have you foremost and front. You deserve and ought yet to be among the first in the hearts of this mighty and armed rebellion.

Without the full measure of devotion which your blood and your valor won. You are the men who, when treason sped her poisoned arrows at the heart of the great Republic, left your homes and dear ones and stood up as a mighty barrier between the government and armed rebellion. Without the full measure of devotion which you unselfishly gave at the proper time and place, in the great extremity, we would not have this grand and glorious country of ours, of which we are this day so justly proud.

In those eventful days we stood hand to hand, shoulder to shoulder, heart to heart, and fought upon many fields of bloody strife. Ties of friendship and association were then formed which nothing but the icy hand of death can destroy or tear asunder.

Our patriotic devotion to our country's flag has also been increased by the mighty sacrifices we have made - by the times we have followed that starry banner through the iron storms and leaden hail. Its stripes remind us of that great price with which our noble ancestors purchased our precious liberties; its beautiful blue galaxy tells us that by the bravery, courage and heroism of our comrades in arms, not one single star fell from that glorious constellation of States.

Almost a quarter of a century has rolled around since the war closed, and you are all growing old. Soon the cold hand of the destroyer will lay hold of you; and though your locks are becoming gray with fast declining years, though your steps are unsteady and your bodily infirmities are fast increasing, all caused by the hardships and privations of a cruel war; yet this we know, that the fires of your lofty patriotism will continue to burn brightly to the end.

You have fought a good fight, you have run the course. May the glory of your mighty deeds, and the cloudy pillar which hovered over all of us upon many a well-fought field, ever keep us in the way of truth and righteousness, and direct us onward and upward to the Promised Land, where we shall enroll ourselves anew in the armies of the Great Ruler who hath given all the victories.

First Lieutenant James A. Gardner
September 11, 1889

Union Veterans Lapel Button

The Union Veteran Legion was founded in Pittsburgh in 1884. It was open only to those who served in the Union forces for at least 3 years and those who had been wounded. It is likely that this button was awarded to Private John Dunnan.

APPENDIX G

ASSOCIATION OF BATTERY B

From: Lawrence County Memoirs: Historical Recollections from Lawrence County Pennsylvania and Surrounding Areas

In April, 1869, the surviving members of Battery B gathered for a reunion in Mount Jackson in what became an annual event. The reunion, usually held at June 8, became a popular event for the community of Mount Jackson and was often attended by other Civil War veterans from around the area. The event – which featured a parade followed by a short veterans meeting and a community picnic – was usually held near the Methodist Church at Nesbit's Grove, a popular picnic area now located in the Jackson Knolls residential area.

In August, 1880, the veterans of the unit erected a small memorial pillar honoring Battery B at Gettysburg, and it was one of the very first monuments to be placed on the historic battlefield. It was placed on East Cemetery Hill, near where the unit held its ground during Pickett's Charge. The pillar was marked with various inscriptions concerning the unit's history. A second and much more impressive monument (topped with a carved cannon), its $1,500 cost made possible by state funding, was erected along the smaller monument on September 11, 1889. Another monument, a large stone tablet marking the unit's position on the first day of action, was erected years later in 1938.

In 1905, during the thirty-six annual reunion, it was first proposed that a monument be erected in Mount Jackson to honor the men of Battery B. Less than a year later Battery B lost its former commander as James H. Cooper passed away in New Castle on March 21, 1906. He was laid to rest in historic Greenwood Cemetery in New Castle. Efforts for the monument continued to gain momentum and fundraising efforts got underway a few years later. During the reunion on June 8, 1911, on the fiftieth anniversary of the beginning of the Civil

War, over 1,000 people took part in the festivities at Nesbit's Grove. A twenty-foot-high monument, to be fashioned in Vermont, was soon authorized. The four sides of the base of the monument would have panels that spelled out the history of the unit. Harry and William Zimmerman of Mount Jackson generously donated a quarter acre lot on the Mount Jackson-New Castle Road for the monument site. After some investigation it was determined the site would require work to get in into shape and a more desirable location was selected adjoining the Methodist Church property. This was a more symbolic location anyway as it was where the unit gathered before heading off to war in 1861.

Work on the foundation for the monument began in late May, 1912, as the completed obelisk was shipped aboard the Pennsylvania Railroad (PRR) to Bessemer. The original plan was to unload the monument at Mahoningtown, but this plan was abandoned for some reason. From Bessemer it was loaded onto large wagons and transported to Mount Jackson over the course of several days. The monument was put in place at the bottom of the large hill where the Methodist Church was situated. The annual reunion was delayed a few weeks to allow the work to be completed.

On Friday, June 28, 1912, during the reunion, the monument was dedicated before a large crowd of onlookers. It was unveiled by William E. Porter, a Lawrence County Judge and President of the Battery B Monument Association, and Mary Cooper, the daughter of Capt. James H. Cooper. The monument sat at the bottom of the large hill where the Methodist Church and its cemetery were situated.

Dedication of the Battery B monument at Mt Jackson, 1912

BATTERY B

In April, 1923, a Civil War-era cannon, provided by the Raritan Arsenal in New Jersey, was acquired to go on display next to the Battery B Monument in Mount Jackson. The 3-inch gun was believed to be an experimental rifled cannon cast in 1863 at the Harry N. Hooper & Company foundry in Boston, Massachusetts. In the Spring of 1926 a campaign was started to relocate the monument and cannon to the top of the hill where the Methodist Church was once located. The cemetery association, which was also officially chartered at about that time, sought to acquire additional properties through several deals.

Ten members of Battery B attended the fiftieth reunion in June, 1919 – in the wake of the Great War (World War I) – while at least one other surviving member was unable to attend. The annual reunions continued throughout the 1920s while the surviving members of Battery B slowly dwindled. The last two members were ninety years old when they died. They were George W. Pitzer of New Castle, who passed away on December 13, 1929, and David P. Needler of Edinburg, the last remaining survivor when he died on November 3, 1930.

http://www.lawrencecountymemoirs.com/lcmpages/178/mount-jackson-cemetery-mount-jackson-pa

QR Code for above URL[77]

---

[77] See footnote 76

**Battery B Monument, Mt. Jackson,
Pennsylvania (2013)**

APPENDIX H

OBITUARY:
CAPTAIN JAMES H. COOPER

New Castle News, March 21, 1906

Captain J.H. Cooper Answered The Last Call This Morning
Gallant Soldier Succumbs After A Long Struggle Against Dread Disease:
"Bravest Man In Army" Passed to Long Rest
Was one of the most distinguished men of The County
And his Death is Regretted by All – Was brave and Very Modest

Captain J. Harvey Cooper "The Bravest Man in The Army of The Potomac" according to the exclamation of admiration by General John F. Reynolds at the second *Battle of Fredericksburg*, passed away at his home on North Jefferson Street about 2:30 o'clock Wednesday morning.

With his passing from life one of the most honored and respected citizens of the county is lost to the community he had so long graced, and intense regret is felt and expressed upon all sides that he has received and answered the long last roll call. No man was held higher esteem than Captain Cooper and every person who knew him justly considered the gallant veteran a friend.

His career as a defender of the Stars & Stripes, his conduct as a man, a citizen and a friend all endeared him to the hearts of the people and his death will long be regretted.

The end was not unexpected for he had been in failing health for some months, suffering from heart weakness. This first became manifest when he was stricken while attending the recent National Encampment of the GAR at Denver last summer. After returning home he recovered to a great extent and was able to be at his place of business as usual, although his strength was not restored.

DAVID BUTT

For some weeks past he had been confined to his home and it was for several days realized that all hope of recovery had passed and the family and friends awaited the end with what resignation they could. The gallant Captain himself also realized this and looked for the peace and hope to rejoining upon the shore the loved ones who had preceded him there.

The record of Captain Cooper in the dark days of the civil war was one that reflects honor upon himself and his gallant men and the entire community that sent them forth.

He was born March 6th 1840 in Allegany County and celebrated the 66th anniversary of his birth the first part of this month. His father was the late George Cooper, one of men of the affairs in Western Pennsylvania during early days, who later settled near Mt. Jackson.

Captain Cooper enlisted with the Mt. Jackson Guards on April 26th, 1861, rushing to arms shortly after Fort Sumter had been fired upon. He was immediately elected First Sergeant; Captain Henry T. Danforth became Captain. The company was mustered into the state service June 8th, 1861, and at Camp Wright, Pittsburgh, was accepted as part of the Light Artillery forces of the commonwealth and became "Battery B" of the first regiment of Pennsylvania Light Artillery.

Captain Cooper was then elected second lieutenant. When the Battery was moved to Harrisburg July 22nd Captain Danforth was promoted to Majorship and Lieutenant Cooper was then elected Captain of the Battery showing his popularity even as a young man.

The Battery was sworn into the United States service August 5th of that year and was immediately sent to Washington and joined the Army of the Potomac, becoming part of the first brigade of General McCall's division of Pennsylvania reserves, commanded by General john F. Reynolds, who met his death on the battlefield at Gettysburg. During the entire civil war Coopers Battery was first and fifth army corps and constituted a part of the Pennsylvania reserves during its service.

Coopers Battery participated in more than 27 engagements that find rank as battles in the pages of history and was fiercely engaged in nine of the 12 great battles of the war, in which the losses reached more than 12000 men, which shows its service. Among the greater battles in which it took part were the *Second Bull Run, Peninsula*

BATTERY B

Campaign, Antietam, the *First* and *Second Battles of Fredericksburg, Chancellorsville*, and the three-day desperate fighting at *Gettysburg, The Wilderness, Spotsylvania, Cold Harbor, North Anna River*, and *Petersburg*. In addition to many others of minor importance, Captain Cooper was mustered out of the service August 8th, 1864, when his term of enlistment expired.

During his service he had several horses shot under him in battle and the service he saw was of the most desperate character. During the second *Battle of Fredericksburg* Coopers Battery alone and single-handed repulsed the confederate counter advance after the union forces had been repulsed. Standing at the "Angle" and firing grape and canister at the advancing horses until they broke and fled after coming within 50 yards of Cooper and his intrepid men. It was one of the most gallant Acts of the entire war and the men of Battery B decided to face capture and death rather than retreat for that would have meant the entire left wing of the Union Army which was then in a desperate plight. General Reynolds realized the gravity of the occasion and the full impact of the Mt. Jackson men's heroism and it was then he galloped up to the Bloody Angle and made the famous exclamation quoted above, which is found in histories of the great conflict.

The Battery lost 21 men in action during the war and had 52 men wounded, although the records show over 100 wounds inflicted upon them. This is because many of the wounded recovered and returned to the service, to be wounded again. The ratio of loss was greater than that of any other volunteer Battery during the entire civil war. Over 11,300 rounds of ammunition were used by the battery which was always in front, owing to the well known coolness and daring of the gallant Captain. He was a personal friend of General Meade and General Reynolds as well as General Hunt, the Chief of Artillery for the Army of the Potomac and was frequently recommended for advancement but refused in order to remain with the Battery and the men he began his service.

He was once commissioned a Major of the first Pennsylvania Light Artillery regiment but declined. Later he was recommended by General Meade for the Colonelcy of the same regiment, but never presented it to the war department and so lost the honor. General Meade's recommendation is now among the Captains private papers.

In his private life he was modest and retiring to such a degree that any honors he received had to be forced upon him against his inclination. He was a member of the First Presbyterian Church and of the patriotic orders of the men who fought in the conflict that almost tore the nation asunder.

He is survived by one daughter, Miss Mary, who resides at home. His wife died many years ago and the gallant captain was the last of his immediate family. His sister Mrs. McElwee of New Wilmington passed away last week, but his condition was then so low that his family feared to inform him of it would be when he met her upon the other shore.

Truly, with the death of Captain James Harvey Cooper this city has lost a citizen of whom the community might well be proud and would have loved to honor far more than it did, had he not declined all matter of the nature.

Funeral services, Friday afternoon at 230 o'clock from the Cooper residence no 173 North Jefferson street. Interment at Greenwood.

http://www.rootsweb.ancestry.com/~palawren/military/_vti_cnf/Obituaries/james_harvey_cooper.htm

QR Code for above URL[78]

---

[78] QR codes are handy "keys" to access internet web sites (URLs) without a computer using a 'smart' phone. QR code *readers* are free downloads on the internet. They enable the interpretation of the two-dimensional pattern of black and white squares as shown above when a 'picture is taken' of that code using a phone with a reader installed. The result is a phone-sized web site whose size of presentation can be controlled manually.

APPENDIX I

CIVIL WAR ARMY ORGANIZATION AND RANK[79]

Organization

A Civil War army consisted of many small parts that were joined together in stair-step fashion to make larger units. There were six basic units of organization. The smallest was a company, which had around 100 men. The largest was an army, which could have many thousands of men.

COMPANY

A company was the basic unit in a Civil War army. A company had approximately 100 men and was commanded by a captain. Companies were named with the letters A–K (*J* was not used because it looked too much like *I*.)

REGIMENT

A regiment usually contained ten companies. A regiment had approximately 1,000 men and was commanded by a colonel. If the unit had only four to eight companies, it was called a battalion rather than a regiment.

BRIGADE

A brigade contained an average of four regiments. A brigade had approximately 4,000 men and was commanded by a brigadier general. Union brigades were named with numbers, but Confederate brigades were often named after their current or former commanding officers.

DIVISION

A division contained three to five brigades. A division had approximately 12,000 men and was commanded by a major general.

---

[79] http://www.townofelbridge.com/Organization%20and%20Rank.pdf

Confederate divisions tended to contain more brigades than their Union counterparts. Confederate divisions often had twice as many men as Union divisions had.

CORPS

A corps contained an average of three divisions. A corps had approximately 36,000 men and was commanded by a major general (Union) or a lieutenant general (Confederate).

ARMY

An army comprised from one to eight corps. An army was commanded by a general. The Union often named its armies after rivers or waterways, i.e., Army of the Potomac. The Confederacy named its armies after states or regions, i.e., Army of Northern Virginia.

Ranks and Responsibilities

The rank of a Civil War soldier indicated his duties and responsibilities within the army. The vast majority of soldiers were enlisted men—they made up the bulk of the fighting force. Above them were noncommissioned officers (also considered enlisted soldiers) and commissioned officers. While officers had more prestige than privates, they also carried added burdens, since they were accountable for all the soldiers under their command.

MAJOR GENERAL

A major general had the command and administrative responsibilities for an infantry division. He had to ensure that his division was well cared for and ready to fight when needed. In battle, he commanded his division by issuing orders to his brigade commanders on where to position their troops.

BRIGADIER GENERAL

A brigadier general had command and administrative duties for an infantry or cavalry brigade, made up usually of four regiments. He had to keep his men in good condition and ready to fight. In battle, he led his brigade by instructing his regiments on where to fight.

COLONEL

A colonel had the command and administrative duties for an infantry, cavalry, or artillery regiment, made up of varying numbers of companies. The colonel was expected to lead his regiment into battle personally to ensure that it performed to its utmost ability. For this reason, colonels were often killed or wounded in action.

LIEUTENANT COLONEL

A lieutenant colonel was the second in command of an infantry, cavalry, or artillery regiment. He had to assist the colonel in all duties, and in battle, he helped lead the regiment into the fight. If the colonel was killed or wounded, the lieutenant colonel immediately took command of the regiment.

MAJOR

A major was third in command of an infantry, cavalry, or artillery regiment and assisted the colonel in administrative and combat duties. In battle, an infantry major led the regimental attack, positioning himself at the front with the color guard. If the colonel and the lieutenant colonel were killed or wounded, the major took command of the regiment.

CAPTAIN

A captain had command of a company of infantry or cavalry, or an artillery battery of guns. In addition to his administrative duties, an infantry captain led his company into battle by giving the proper commands for the movement and fighting of his troops, in concert with the other companies in the regiment.

LIEUTENANT

Lieutenants were second in command of infantry and cavalry companies and artillery batteries. Infantry lieutenants assisted the company captain in their positions behind the line of battle by guiding the troops in their movements and firing.

SERGEANT MAJOR

A sergeant major was a regimental staff member responsible for keeping reports for the regiment. In battle, he advanced on the left, behind the line of battle, to help guide troop movement.

SERGEANT

Sergeants served either in the regimental color guard or in the individual companies of the regiment. There could be divisions, related to administrative duties, within the rank—for example, first sergeant, ordnance sergeant, and quartermaster sergeant. Infantry sergeants advanced either in or behind the line of battle, depending on individual responsibilities. They helped guide troop movements and kept the men in position by example and force of command.

CORPORAL

Corporals served either in the regimental color guard or individual companies of the regiment. During combat, infantry corporals who were not part of the color guard were positioned in the line of battle. They helped to keep a uniform line in movement of the company. Privates looked to corporals to help guide them during combat.

PRIVATE

Privates served as the backbone of the army and did most of the fighting. Privates moved together shoulder to shoulder in straight battle lines and acted on the commands of their company officers. Privates rarely acted independently but rather worked as a group with the single purpose of fighting as a sheer force of numbers.

In addition to the regular ranks, Civil War armies had several specialist ranks. Each regiment had a contingent of staff officers, which included surgeons, quartermasters, adjutants, and, on occasion, chaplains. There were also special ranks for soldiers in specific parts of a regiment, such as the field music (fife and drums), the regimental band (brass instruments and drums), and the color guard. The color guard was an honorary group chosen to carry the flag, or colors, of the regiment. It usually consisted of eight color corporals and one color sergeant.

APPENDIX J

ORDERS OF BATTLE: SEVEN DAYS BATTLES

Federal:

http://en.wikipedia.org/wiki/Seven_Days_Union_order_of_battle

QR Code for above URL

Confederate:

http://en.wikipedia.org/wiki/seven_Days_Confederate_order_of_battle

QR Code for above URL

The Battle of Malvern Hill - watercolor by artist Robert Knox Sneden. Confederate troops attacking up the hill were decimated by artillery from both the top of the hill and from gunboats on the James River.

General John H. Martindale (seated) near Richmond

Drawing by Waud of the last battle of the Pennsylvania Reserves at the Battle of Spottsyvania Court House in May 1864.

Alanson Randol, who was brought into McCall's depleted Pennsylvanian Reserves and fought beside Battery B at Glendale

Heintzelman and staff at Harrisons Landing

INDEX - boldface indicates illustration or map

A

Aqueduct
　Aqueduct Bridge · 7, 11, **12**
Army Corps
　I Corps · xxxi, 44, 48-51
　II Corps · 44, 50, 67, 78, 90, 100, 105, 110, 111
　III Corps · 44, 57, 64, 76, 103, 105, 130, 131, 134
　IV Corps · 27, 44, 50, 63, 66, 78, 110
　V Corps · xxxii, 64, 66, 68, 78, 88, 89, 95, 102, 103, 120
　VI Corps · 27, 51, 63, 66, 78, 90, 93, 99, 105
Army Organization and Rank · 171
Artillery - **xv**
　Howitzer · 41, **42**
　Parrott Rifles · 18, **19**
　Quaker Guns · **47**

B

Balloon
　Lowe, T.S.C. · 16, **17**, 90
Battery B · xii, xiv, xviii, xix, xx, xxi, xxiii, **xxiv, xxv,** xxvi, xxix, xxx, xxxi, xxxii, 13, 18, 19, 32, 37, 51, **54,** 72, 80, 82-83, **87**-88, 94, 107, 108
Battery B, Cooper ·*See also* Cooper iv, vii, xii, xv, xviii, xix, xx, xxiii, **xxiv, xxv,** xxvi, 1, **14,** 21, 44, 67, 69, 78, 80, 82, 86, 87, 94, 96, 98, 105, 111, 117, **118**, 134, 135, 145, 146, 155, 156, 157, 168, 169
Battery B Association · viii, 137, 163
Battery B Monument Dedication - 145-162, 166
Battles
　Ball's Bluff · 21, 34, 35, **36**
　Bull Run/Manassas · xix, xx, xxiii, xxvii, xxviii, xxix, 4, 7, 8, 16, 21, 27, 37, **48**, 51, 84, 115, 117, 127, 129, 131, 134, 135, 139, 142, 143, 144, 147, 168
　Dranesville · xxxi, 10, 21, 29, 60, 142, 146
　Drewry's Bluff - 57
　Fair Oaks *See also Seven Pines* · 66, 67
　Hanover Courthouse · **65,** 66
　Mechanicsville · 17, 78, 86
　Philippi Races · 4
　Port Republic - 60
　Rich Mountain - 4
　Seven Pines · 17, 66, 76
　Williamsburg - 55, 57
Seven Days Battles
　Beaver Dam Creek/ Mechanicsville · 72, 75, 76, 78, 79, 80, 84, 85, **87**, 88, 89, 91
　Gaines's Mill · vii, xxxii, 17, 87, 88, 89, 94, **96, 97,** 98, 99, 105, 108, 121
　Garnett's and Golding's Farm · vii, 99
　Glendale · xxxii, 102, **118, 120,** 129, 142, 143, 144
　Malvern Hill · xxxii, 102, 103, 112, 113, 117, 120, 124, 142, **176**
　Oak Grove · 76, 78
　Savage's Station - 100-**101**

C

Camps
　Camp Barry · **xv**, xxxi, 1
　Camp Curtin - xx, xxxi
　Camp Pierpont · xxxi, 19, 21, 22, 33, 37
　Camp Wilks - 34
　Camp Wright · xx, xxvii, xxxi, 168
　Camp Tenally · xxxi, 1, **2**
Casualties · xxvi, xxviii, xxix, 57, 58, 65, 67, 77, 83, 84, 90, 91, 92, 93, 94, 95, 99, 100, 109, 112, 117, 120, 121, 123, 125, 126, 146, 148, 160
Confederate Officers
　Alexander, E. Porter ·108, 114
　Anderson, J. - 81, **85**, 91, 147
　Anderson, R. · 92, 107
　Archer, James · 82, **85**, 149, 154
　Beauregard, P.G.T. · xxvii
　Branch, Lawrence · 80, 91, **92**

Davis, Jefferson (Confederate
  President) · 68, 106
Evans, Nathan G. · 22, 84, **85**
Ewell, Richard, S. - 59, 61, 91
Field, Charles W. · 82, 91, 147
Gregg, Maxcy · 91, **92**
Hill, A. P. · 78, **79**, 80, 81, 82, 83, 84,
  85, 88, 91, 92, 103, 104, 106, 109,
  110, 149
Hill, D. H. · 78, **79**, 83, 93, 120
Holmes, Theophilus · 103, 106
Hood, John B. · 93, **97**, 115
Huger, Benjamin · 76, **77**, 79, 103,
  105, 106, 110, 111
Jackson, Thomas (Stonewall) · 50,
  53, 54, **55**, 59, 60, **61**, 76, 78, 79,
  80, 82, 90, 92, 93, 94, 103, 105,
  106 , 111, 134, 147, 148,
Jenkins, Micah · **107**, 111, 112
Johnston, Joseph E. · xxvii, 38, 39, 45,
  46, 47, 50, 52, 56, 57, 64, 66, 67,
  68
Kemper, James · **107**, 110, 111, 112
Lee, Robert E. · 17, 60, 66, **68**, 74, 76,
  78, 79, 82, 85, 93, 95, 100, 103,
  106, 111, 113, 114, 120, 121, 127,
  128, 130, 132, 147, 154, 158
Longstreet, James · 78, 79, 92, 103,
  104, 106, 107, 110, 112, 114, 147,
  149, 157
Magruder, John · **56**, 57, 79, 100,
  103, 106
Pegram, William J. · 81, 149
Pender, W. Dorsey · 83, 91, 147, 151
Ripley, Roswell · 83, **85** 147
Stuart, J.E.B. · 29, 52
Whiting, W.H.C. · 93, 97
Wilcox, Cadmus · 92, **107**, 109, 112,
  157
Winder, Charles S. · 93
Confederate President
  Jefferson Davis - 68, 106

D

Disease · 40, 41, 54, 72, 121-125 135,
  138, 139, 161
Dunnan Soldiers - 137, 141
  Hugh · 138, 139, 140
  James - 138
  John · xiii, 137, **162**
  Official Army Records · **141**

Robert · **xii,** xiii, xiv, xvi, xvii, xxvix,
  xxxi, 5, 101, 123, 124, 139, 140,
  141, 143
Samuel · 137, 140, 141

E

Edward's Ferry - 27, 28, 42
Ellerson's Mill - **87,** 106, 107, **113**

F

Falmouth · xxxi, 53, 70
Flag of the 1st Artillery Regiment ·
  xviii, 89, 131, 174
Fredericksburg · xxxi, 54, 61, 68, 69,
  142, 148, 169

G

Gettysburg
  Dedication of Battery B Monument ·
    130, 142, 145-162,
Glendale National Cemetery · 124
Grapevine Bridge · 67, **97**
Great Falls · xxxi, 9, **10,** 13, 22

H

Harrisons Landing - **xxxii,** 75, 90, 112,
  120-**124**

I

Injuries · 40, 94, 124, **126,** 135
Iron clad ships · xxix, 58

L

Leesburg · 10, 21, 27, 37, 48
Letter from Samuel Dunnan · **140**
Light Artillery of Pennsylvania
  Reserves · xiv, 29

Lincoln, A. (President Abraham Lincoln) · xvi, xvii, xxii, xxviii, 4, 6, 8, 10, 15, 20, 21, 35, 37, 42, 43, 45, 47, 48, 50, 51, 53, 54, 59, 60, 127, **128,**
Lowe, Thaddeus S.C. · 16, 17

M

Manassas *See also* Bull Run
McCown, Willard Dunnan · iii, xiii
Mt Jackson (Lawrence County Seat) · xii, xiii, xvi, xvii, xviii, xix, xx, xxi, 54, 84, 112, 124, 133, 137, **166**

N

New Castle, Pennsylvania · viii, xvi, 123, 163, 165, 167

O

Obituary, Cooper
  New Castle News · 167
Old Tavern · 76, 78, 85

P

Palmetto Sharpshooters Regiment · 107, 108, 112
Peninsula Campaign Part 1 · 55
Peninsula Campaign Part 2 · 63
Peninsula Campaign Part 3 · 76
Pennsylvania Governor
  Andrew Curtin · xx, xxiii, 15, 25, 132, 135
Pennsylvania Reserves · xviii, xx, xxii, xxiii, xxvi, xxx, xxxi, xxxii, 1, 5, 13, 21, 25, 29, 51, 69, 79, 80, 92, 107, 117, 120, 130, 134, 146, 147, 153, **177**
Pennsylvania Volunteers · v, xix, xxvi, 81

R

Railroad
  Baltimore and Ohio · 3
  Loudoun and Hampshire · 48
  Manassas Gap Railroad · 59, 139
  Orange and Alexandria - 45, 52, 158
  Pennsylvania Railroad · 164
  Richmond and York Railroad - 66
  Virginia Central Railroad - 65
  Weldon Railroad · 142, 159
Richmond · xv, xxvii, xxxii, 8, 38, 40, 45, 46, 47, 50, 51, 53, 54, 65, 66, 68, 69, 73, 76, 77, 78, 79, 85, 88, 95, 103, 114, 121, 123, 127
Rivers
  Allegheny · 68
  Chickahominy · 65, 66, 78, 83, 94, **97**
  James · 46, 57, 66, 88, 95, 100, 102, 103, 113, 120, 122, 127, **139**
  Pamunkey · 66, **72,** 88
  Potomac · xxxi, 1, 7, 9, 19, 50
  Rappahannock · 37, 38, 53, 65
  York Rivers · 50, 57, 66, 70
Roll of Honor · viii, 143, 144

S

Secession · xvi, xxii, 7
Secretary of War
  Simon Cameron · 32
  Edwin Stanton · xiv, **38,** 39, 47, 51, 53, 69
Seneca Falls · xxxi, 33
Seven Days Battles - 76 *See also* Battles
Shenandoah Valley · xxvii, 50, 54, **56,** 58, 59, 60, 66, 76, 79
Ships - 49, 72, 106
  CSS Virginia - 46, 47, 57, 58
  GWP Custis - 17
  Hamor · 70
  Iron Clad - 46, 47, 57, 58
  USS Galena - 57, 58, 103
  USS. Monitor · 47, **58**
Sickness - *See also* disease
Surgeon Jonathan Letterman - 123

U

Union Officers
  Amsden, Frank P. · 105, 107, 108
  Baker, Edward Dickinson · 23, 35
  Banks, Nathaniel P. · 1, 32, 33, 45, 48, 50, 53, 54, 59, 60

Barry, William · 1, **26**
Biddle, Chapman · 149, 150, 151, 152, 153
Biddle, Henry - 43
Burns, William W. · · 110
Butterfield, Daniel · 91, 92, **95**
Cadwalader, Thomas · 13, 80, 86, 102, 112, 143
Caldwell, John C. · 110
Campbell, Charles T. · · 24
Colburn, Albert V. · **126**
Cooper, James H. · **xxi**, xxiv, xxv, 13, 14, 30, 37, 71, 80, 81, 82, 83, 86, 87, 88, 89, 94, 96, 98, 105, 107, 108, 109, 111, 112, 116, 117, 120, 131, 133-137, 145, 148, 150, 153, 154, 156, 157, 158, 159, 163, 164, 167-170
Custer, George Armstrong · 52
Cuthbertson, John · 107
Danforth, Henry ·xix, xx, xxi, 2, 80, 86, 102, 112, 133, 143, 146, 168
De Hart, Henry V. · 71, 80, 89, 94, 115
Diederich, Otto · 105, 110
Easton, Hezekiah · 29, 30, 71, 80, 89, 93, 115
Franklin, William B. · 51, **63**, 78, 90, 99, 105, 114,
Gardner, James A. · v, xix, 145-162
Grant. Ulysses S. · 128, 130
Griffin, Charles · 91. **95**
Heintzelman, Samuel · **44**, 76, 77, 78, 103, 105, 114, **177**
Hooker, Joseph · 57, 76, 103, **104,** 105, 106, 110, 113, 130, 132, 148
Hunt, Henry · **120**, 135, 157, 169
Jackson, C. Feger - **108**, 131
Kearny, Phillip · 76, 103, **104**, 105, 110, 114
Kern, Mark · 28, 71, 80, 81, 82, 83, 89, 93, 105, 115
Keyes, Erasmus · **44**, 63, 66, 78
Martindale, John · 81, 91, **95, 176**
McCall, George A · xxiii, xxvi, xxv, xxxi, xxxii, 1, 5, **6,** 9, 13, 19, 21, 22, 24, 25, 30, 31, 32, 37, 43, 44, 51, 54, 60, **64**, 69, 71, 78, 79, 82, 84, 88, 89, 90, 93, 94, 95, 97, 98, 102-106, 109-114, **116**, 117, 120, 121, 129, 131, 146, 147, 168
McCandless, William · 81, **82**
McClellan, George B. · **vi**, xxviii, **3**, 8, 10, 15, 20, 21, 26, 27, 32, 35, 37 38, 39,, 42, 43, 45-49, 50, 51, 53, 54, 56, 57, 59, 60, 61, 63, 65-69, 72, 73, 74, 76-79, 85, 88, 90, 95, 100, 103, 113, 120, 121, 127, **128,** 129, 135
McDowell, Irvin · xxvii, xxviii, 4, **44**, 48, 49, 50, 51, 53, 54, 59, 60, 63, 65, 66, 69, 130, 131, 134, 146
McIntosh, John B. · 52
Meade, George G. · 21, **24, 25**, 29, 31, 44, 71, 81, 83, 89, 104, 105, 109, 111, 129-**131**, 132, 134, 135, 148, 158, 169
Meredith, Solomon · 133, 149, 152,
Morrell, George W. · **64**, 78, 79, 81, 89, 91, 95
Ord, Edward O. C. · 29, **31**, 60, 89
Patterson, Robert · xxiii, xxviii
Porter, Fitz John · **ix**, **64**, 65, 66, 68, 78, 79, 82, 88, 89, 90, 93, 94, 102, 120, 121, 124, 146
Randol, Alanson · **105,** 107, 108, 109, **177**
Reynolds, John F. · xxx, 2, 5, **6,** 29, 31, 32, 44, 61, 62, 79, 80, 81, 82, 84, 86, 89, 93, 95, 96, 105, 110, 111, 130, 131-**133**, 134, 146-149, 153, 167, 168, 169
Sackett. Delos B. · **126**
Sedgwick, John · 105, 106, 110, **111**, **126**
Seymour, Truman · 44, **45**, 71, 80, 83, 84, 86, 89, 90, 104, 105, 108, 110, 111, 112, 131
Shields, James · 54, 60
Simmons, Seneca · **105**, 110, 111
Slocum, Henry · **63**, 90, 93, 95, 105
Smead, John R. · 80, 82, 83
Smith, William · 1, 27, **63,** 99, 105, 106, **124**
Stone, Charles · 21, 22, **23**, 24, 32, 33, 34, **35**, 36
Stone, Roy - **82**, 149, 150, 153
Stoneman, George · 52
Sumner, Edwin V. · **44**, 50, 67, 78, 90, 94, 100, 105, 110
Sykes, George · **64**, 78, 89, 91
Union Soldiers
  Angus, David B. · 84, 85
  Bear, James K.M. · 20
  Bender, George - 37

181

Brubach, David · 112
Buchanan, Joseph · 112
Chambers, Robert - 54, 143
Davis, Cyrus W. · 112
Duff, Hernando - 54, 143
Dunnan, Hugh - xvi, 138
Dunnan, James - xvi, i37
Dunnan, John - xiv, 137, 141
Dunnan, Robert · xiii, xiv, xvi, xvii, xxix, xxxi, 5, 80, 123, 124, 140, 141, 143
Dunnan, Samuel · xvi, xvii, 137, 140
Elwell, Charles - 54, 143
Flaxenhart, Peter G. - 85
Fravel, William · 112
Frew, David W. - 54
Fullerton, James - 41
Fullerton, John - 41
Fullerton, Walter - 41
Germer, A. H. - 40
Hamill, John S. · 112
Hughston, John C. - 54, 143
Johnston, Franklin · 112, 144
Kennedy, Robert (Albert) · 112
Lamm, John · 85
McClurg, James M. - 16, 144
McGinnis, Alvin - 27, 40
McGinnis, George - 27
McGinnis, James - 27, 54, 144
McGinnis, Samuel - 27
McWilliams, Theodore - 54
Meanor, John A. · 85
Miller, James S. · 112, 143
Nesbit, Isaac A. - 49
Nesbit, James T. · 49, 84
Officer, William - 41
Osborn, Charles - 31
Penrod, John T. - 34
Runshaw, John W. · 28
Seifert, Frederick B. - 20, 144
Smoot, Edward · 84, 144
Tait, Thomas W. · 84, 144
Waldron, William N. · 112, 144
Wallace, William W. · 112
Weir, John N. - 40
Wilson, Isaac P. · 112, 144

V

Valley
  The Valley Campaign Part 1 · 50
  The Valley Campaign Part 2 · 59

W

Washington · xiii, xvi, xvii, xx, xxii, xxiii, xxvi, xxix, xxxi, 1, 2, 4, **7-12**, 15, 17, 18, 21, 22, 33, 35, 37, 41, 42, 43, 45, 46, 48, 50, 51, 59, 60, 61, 69, 89, 103, 121, 127, 135, 139, 146, 157, 168
White House Landing · xxxii, 66, 69, **71, 72,** 78, 88
White Oak Creek · 99
White Oak Swamp · xxxii, 76, 100, 102, 103, 105, 106, 111, **115**
Williamsburg · 55, 57, 66
Winchester · 50, 59

Y

Yorktown · 17, 50, 55, 56, 57, 66, 69

Z

Zeppelin - 17

David Butt is a former journalist who has worked for a considerable time at senior levels in the Australian health system. He is a keen but occasional writer of fiction, and a latent student of the Civil War, as demonstrated by the interest aroused by Robert Dunnan's war diary.

www.ingramcontent.com/pod-product-compliance
Lightning Source LLC
Chambersburg PA
CBHW031953080426

42735CB00007B/372